CW01024599

THE **A9**
HANDBOOK

First published in Great Britain 2024 by
Posthouse Publishing, No 2 Cleat, St Margaret's Hope,
South Ronaldsay, Orkney, KW17 2RW

Text © Posthouse Publishing and Gavin D. Smith

A CIP catalogue for this book is available from the British Library
ISBN 978 1 903872 390
10 9 8 7 6 5 4 3 2 1

Disclaimer: The publishers have made every effort to ensure the accuracy of information in
the book at the time of going to press. However, they cannot accept responsibility for any loss,
injury or inconvenience resulting from the use of information contained in this book.

Design by Helloideas
Printed and bound in Great Britain

Dedication
To the memory of my grandfather, Matthew Dick Smith (1896-1976)

Acknowledgements
Quote on front cover John Rebus Ltd, Visit Scotland © pages viii/ix, 15, 21, 29, 31, 34/35, 40,
58/59, 64/65, 71, 74, 85, 86/87, 91, 95, 99, 103, 104/105, 110/111, 114, 124/125, 129, 132/133, 172, 177,
185, Uile-Bheist distillery for page 127, Ian Mcleod Distillers Ltd 26/27, Flickr, 13, 16/17, 22/23,
44, 50/51, 52/53, 55, 61, 76/77, 80/81, 97, all images on 109, 116/117, 145, 158/159, 164, 170, 176,
Dunnet Bay distillery 187.

THE A9 HANDBOOK

A PRACTICAL GUIDE ON HOW TO TRAVEL AND EXPLORE THIS CLASSIC ROAD

GAVIN D. SMITH

Contents

SECTION 1: POLMONT TO PERTH

Bo'ness 12
Kinneil House 12
The Bo'ness & Kinneil Railway and Museum
  of Scottish Railways 14
Bo'ness Motor Museum 14
Blackness Castle 14
Linlithgow Palace 16
Linlithgow distillery 18
Falkirk 19
BREAK OUT: WADE & TELFORD 20
Callendar House 24
The Two Battles of Falkirk 24
Rosebank distillery 26
Falkirk distillery 27
Rough Castle Experiences 28
School of Witchcraft & Potions 29
Falkirk Wheel 29
The Helix and the Kelpies 30
Bannockburn Battlefield 32
The City of Stirling 33
Stirling Castle 34
Argyll's Lodgings 36
Old Town Jail 37
Holy Rude Church 37
Stirling Gin Distillery 38
Stirling Old Bridge 38
Battle of Stirling Bridge 39
National Wallace Monument 40
Cambuskenneth Abbey 42
Blair Drummond Safari Park 43
Doune and Deanston Distillery 45
Deanston Distillery 45
Allanwater Brewhouse 47
Dunblane 48
The Battle of Sheriffmuir 50
Tullibardine distillery 51
Auchterarder 53
Gleneagles 54
Perth 55

RSGS at the Fair Maid's House 57
Perth Museum & Art Gallery 58
Fergusson Gallery 59
Perth Distillery Company 60
The River Tay Public Art Trail 60
Black Watch Castle & Museum 61
Willowgate Activity Centre 62
Branklyn Garden 62
Huntingtower 63
Elcho Castle 63
Scone Palace 65
Perth Racecourse 67

SECTION 2: PERTH TO INVERNESS

Birnam and Dunkeld 70
Beatrix Potter Exhibition and Garden 70
Dunkeld Cathedral 71
The Battle of Dunkeld 72
The Little Houses 72
Dunkeld House Tree Trail 73
The Hermitage 73
Loch of the Lowes 75
Aberfeldy 77
Aberfeldy Distillery 79
Blair Athol Distillery, Pitlochry 82
Pitlochry 83
Pitlochry Dam Visitor Centre 84
Pitlochry Festival Theatre 84
Enchanted Forest 86
Edradour Distillery 88
Queen's View and Killiecrankie 89
Blair Atholl 92
Atholl Country Life Museum 92
Water Mill and Tea Room 93
Wasted Degrees Brewing 93
Blair Castle 94
House of Bruar 97
Clan Donnachaidh Centre,
  & the Falls of Bruar 98
Dalwhinnie Distillery 100
Newtonmore and Kingussie 102
Clan Macpherson Museum 102
Highland Folk Museum 103
Ruthven Barracks 105
Speyside Distillery 106

Highland Wildlife Park	107	Dunrobin Castle	161
BREAK OUT: SCOTTISH WILDLIFE	**108**	Clynelish and Brora distilleries	163
Aviemore and Carrbridge	113	Helmsdale	164
Rothiemurchus	113	Ord of Caithness, Badbea and Berriedale	166
Glenmore Lodge	113	Dunbeath	167
Glenmore Forest Park	115	Dunbeath Heritage Centre	168
Cairngorm Mountain Ski Area	115	The Laidhay Croft Museum	168
The Strathspey Railway	116	Thurso	169
The Snug	117	Wolfburn distillery	170
Cairngorm Brewery	117	North Point Distillery	171
Aviemore Kart Raceway	118	Scrabster	172
Landmark Forest Adventure Park	119	Clan Gunn Heritage Centre & Museum	174
Tomatin Distillery	121	Lybster	174
Culloden Battlefield	122	The Waterlines Heritage Centre	174
Inverness and Loch Ness	123	Grey Cairns of Camster	175
Inverness Museum and Art Gallery	125	Whaligoe Steps	175
Inverness Castle	125	Wick	176
Uile-bheist Distillery	126	The Castle of Old Wick, Sinclair	
Abertarff House	128	& Girnigoe	178
Inverness Botanic Gardens	128	Pulteney distillery	179
Eden Court	129	The Caithness Broch Centre	182
Inverness Victorian Market	129	8 Doors Distillery	183
BREAK OUT: CLANS & TARTANS	**130**	The Castle of Mey	187
The Northern Meeting	134	Dunnet Bay distillery	188
Inverness Highland Games	134	The Seadrift Centre	189
SECTION 3: INVERNESS TO THURSO		Bibliography	190
		Newspapers	190
Inverness	138	Index	191
Glen Ord distillery	139		
Beauly and Dingwall	140		
Black Isle Brewery	142		
The Clootie Well	142		
Alness and Invergordon	143		
Dalmore distillery	145		
Tain	147		
Glenmorangie distillery	149		
BREAKOUT: SCOTCH WHISKY	**150**		
Balblair distillery	154		
Dornoch	155		
Historylinks Museum	156		
Dornoch Cathedral	156		
Dornoch distillery	157		
Royal Dornoch Golf Club	158		
Dornoch Beach	158		
The Mound and Golspie	159		

Preface

My first journey on the A9 was during the summer of 1961. I have to admit that it didn't make a great impression on me, but in my defence, I was only eight months old.

My family lived in north-east England, but my paternal grandfather hailed from Reiss, just outside Wick in Caithness, and I was taken north to be shown off to relatives in Scotland's Far North.

In those days, a car journey from County Durham to Wick was quite an undertaking, involving at least two overnight stops, whereas it can now be accomplished in around seven and a half hours.

The 1970s saw increasing traffic using the A9, particularly during holiday periods, and with no bypasses, every village and town suffered traffic jams. The memory of sitting several miles south of Perth in a baking hot, motionless Hillman Hunter without air-conditioning while wearing a Bri-Nylon shirt, and trousers constructed from an equally sweat-inducing man-made material, remain with me to this day.

Between Perth and Inverness, major 1970s upgrades to by-pass almost all communities made travelling on the A9 altogether more pleasant, though north of Inverness, while some towns have also been by-passed, much of the A9 remains little changed since those sweaty summer teenage trips north.

Overall, the experience of driving on the A9 is vastly different, however, thanks partly to road improvements and partly to ever more sophisticated vehicles. What I celebrate every time I take to the wheel on the 'Great Road North' is that the scenery remains as awe-inspiring as ever and there are many more attractions to visit within proximity of the road than ever before.

Explore and enjoy!

Gavin D. Smith
May 2024

Introduction

'Scotland's Spine,' 'Scotland's Great Road North,' or Scotland's Route 66'. These are all terms that have been applied to the A9 which in its present configuration stretches for 273 miles, making it the longest road in the country.

The A9 followed the route of many much older roads, with sections in the Highlands dating back to the 18th century (see Wade and Telford, p.20). It runs from the old industrial heartland of Scotland past historic cities such as Stirling, Perth and Inverness, before ending up where the road runs out and the Pentland Firth beckons at the port of Scrabster, with the Orkney Islands visible in the distance.

The A9 has great strategic importance as it is one of only three trunk roads directly linking the Lowlands with the Highlands, the others being the A82 from Glasgow to Inverness, via Fort William and the A90 from Edinburgh to Fraserburgh, via Dundee and Aberdeen. North of Inverness, the A9 is really the only game in town, with alternative access to the 'Far North' coming via minor roads and much lengthier and significantly more time-consuming routes to the west.

The 'A9' designation was first applied as part of the formal classification of roads in Great Britain, published on 1st April 1923. The initial route began at the Corstorphine junction in Edinburgh's west end, branching north off the A8, and travelled north to Inverness via Linlithgow, Falkirk, Stirling, Perth, Pitlochry and Kingussie. The road was extended from Inverness to John O'Groats in 1936.

Early drafts of the A9 had the road running from Edinburgh to Queensferry, Inverkeithing, Cowdenbeath and Kinross to Perth, but this was subsequently dropped on favour of the route as noted above, as the draft versions included a ferry crossing of the River Forth, as the Forth Road Bridge did not open until 1964.

With the development of the M9 motorway during the late 1960s/early 1970s, the section of A9 from Edinburgh to Falkirk was reclassified, with the road then commencing at Cadger's Brae, near Polmont, between Grangemouth and Falkirk.

The 1970s also saw the largest scale changes made to the A9 in its entire history. During that deacade, an ambitious programme of civil engineering to bypass towns and villages between Perth

▲ *Dornoch beach.*

and Inverness was instituted, with settlements such as Dunkeld, Pitlochry, Dalwhinnie, Newtonmore, Kingussie and Aviemore all being removed from the route of the A9.

Concerns from local business owners led to an agreement that no roadside developments would be allowed along the road meaning that travellers wishing to avail themselves of services had to leave the A9 and patronise existing local traders. Additionally, Inverness itself was bypassed, along with towns such as Beauly, Dingwall, Alness and Bonar Bridge, while new bridges were constructed across the Beauly, Cromarty and Dornoch firths.

Incremental changes and upgrades mean that today the A9 is single carriageway from its starting point to Dunblane, dual carriageway from Dunblane to Perth, a mix of single carriageway and dual carriageway from Perth to Inverness and single carriageway from just north of Inverness to Scrabster.

The situation should improve to an even greater extent when the programme to make the entire Perth to Inverness section of the A9 dual carriageway is completed. The road project, which was part of the Scottish National Party's 2007 election manifesto, is officially due to be finished in 2025, and includes a £3 billion budget, with work taking place on 11 separate sections covering a total of 80 miles. However, the most likely completion date to have the Perth to Inverness A9 fully dualled has been pushed back to 2035 at the earliest. A campaign group has been formed to push for the Scottish Government to honour its commitment to dual the A9 – see A9 Dual Action Group – #DualtheA9.

USEFUL WEBSITES

Petrol stations: www.fuelgenie.co.uk
Electric vehicle charging points: - www.zap-map.com
Travel information: www.trafficscotland.org

SECTION ONE
Polmont to Perth

Bo'ness	12	Battle of Stirling Bridge	39
Kinneil House	12	National Wallace Monument	40
The Bo'ness & Kinneil Railway		Cambuskenneth Abbey	42
and Museum of Scottish Railways	14	Blair Drummond Safari Park	43
Bo'ness Motor Museum	14	Doune	45
Blackness Castle	14	Deanston Distillery	45
Linlithgow Palace	16	Allanwater Brewhouse	47
Linlithgow distillery	18	Dunblane	48
Falkirk	19	The Battle of Sheriffmuir	50
BREAK OUT; WADE & TELFORD	20	Tullibardine distillery	51
Callendar House	24	Auchterarder	53
The Two Battles of Falkirk	24	Gleneagles	54
Rosebank distillery	26	Perth	55
Falkirk distillery	27	RSGS at the Fair Maid's House	57
Rough Castle Experiences	28	Perth Museum & Art Gallery	58
School of Witchcraft & Potions	29	Fergusson Gallery	59
Falkirk Wheel	29	Perth Distillery Company	60
The Helix and the Kelpies	30	The River Tay Public Art Trail	60
Bannockburn Battlefield	32	Black Watch Castle & Museum	61
The City of Stirling	33	Willowgate Activity Centre	62
Stirling Castle	34	Branklyn Garden	62
Argyll's Lodgings	36	Huntingtower	63
Old Town Jail	37	Elcho Castle	63
Holy Rude Church	37	Scone Palace	65
Stirling Gin Distillery	38	Perth Racecourse	67
Stirling Old Bridge	38		

POLMONT – STIRLING – 15 MILES
STIRLING TO PERTH – 37 MILES

TOTAL DISTANCE – 52 MILES

The section of the A9 between Polmont and Perth transports the traveller from the heart of the old industrial belt of Central Scotland via the historically rich and strategically important city of Stirling to the equally heritage-rich city of Perth, where the Scottish Highlands beckon.

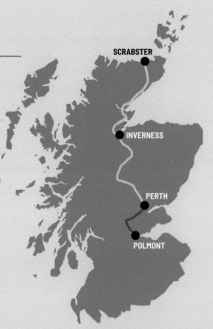

WHERE TO STAY

Hotels

Stirling
Stirling Highland Hotel
stirlinghighlandhotel.co.uk
Premier Inn
premierinn.com
Dunblane
Westlands Hotel
westlandshoteldunblane.co.uk
Gleneagles
gleneagles.com
Perth
The Royal George Hotel
theroyalgeorgehotel.co.uk
Premier Inn
premierinn.com

Caravan/Glamping/Campsites

Stirling area
Blair Drummond Caravan Park
blairdrummondcaravanpark.co.uk
Mains Farm
mainsfarmwigwams.com
Bramble Bield
bramblebield.com
Perth area
Perth Caravan Park
perthcaravanpark.co.uk
Gallowhill Camping & Caravan Park
gallowhillcc.com
5 Roads Caravan Park
5roads.co.uk/

BO'NESS

5.7 MILES FROM POLMONT VIA THE A904

Boristown Ness [sic], a long town, of one street, and no more, extended along the shore, close to the water. It has been, and still is, a town of the greatest trade to Holland and France, before the Union, of any in Scotland, except Edinburgh; and, for shipping, it has more ships belong to it than to Edinburgh and Leith put together; yet their trade is declin'd of late by the Dutch trade, being carry'd on so much by way of England."

Daniel Defoe - A tour thro' the whole island of Great Britain - 1724

Borrowstounness, to give the town its full name, is located on the south bank of the River Forth, 2 miles north of the historic burgh of Linlithgow (see p.16). It was developed as a port for the export of coal during the early 15th century and soon became a prosperous place, with the production of salt, iron and whisky all adding to its significance in the centuries to follow.

Long prior to this, in AD 142, Roman Emperor Antoninus Pius had ordered the construction of a wall to protect the northern extremity of his empire, stretching 37 miles from the River Clyde in the west to the River Forth in the east. The Antonine Wall passed through what is now Bo'ness and the remains – in the shape of a partially excavated fort – may be seen on the Kinneil Estate (see below); many other traces can still be found.

KINNEIL HOUSE

⌂ Provost Rd, Bo'ness ✆ +44 (0) 1620 892727
☉ historicenvironment.scot

Kinneil House is situated to the west of Bo'ness. Work on the present mansion began in 1553 on the orders of James Hamilton, 2nd Lord Hamilton, 1st Earl of Arran. Hamilton had been appointed regent of Scotland 10 years earlier, on the death of King James V, and the lands of Kinneil had been in the hands of the powerful Hamilton family since 1323.

James Hamilton oversaw the construction of what is now the north wing of Kinneil House, complete with two suites of rooms that owed much in design to the royal residences of nearby Linlithgow Palace (see p.16) and Stirling Castle (see p.34).

The late 1670s saw Anne, Duchess of Hamilton, and her husband William start to transform the house into a grand residence for their son James, the Earl of Arran, creating a five-storey tower

▲ *Kinneil House.*

and four-storey 'pavilions' adjoining the tower, and providing a link to the lodgings block. The work took 20 years to complete.

As the Hamilton family's wealth increased due to growing income from coal mined on their lands and other sources, Kinneil House no longer served as their principal seat, and during the late 18th century, Dr John Roebuck, founder of the Carron ironworks, occupied the property.

While Roebuck was in residence, Kinneil earned a little-known but important place in engineering history as it was in a workshop behind the house that James Watt worked from 1769 to 1773, developing his ground-breaking steam engine. The remains of Watt's workshop can still be seen.

In 1936 Bo'ness Town Council started to demolish Kinneil House, and it was only saved by the discovery of 16th-century murals, considered of important historical value. Today, Kinneil House is a Category A listed building in the care of Historical Environment Scotland and open to the public on a limited number of days each year.

THE BO'NESS & KINNEIL RAILWAY AND MUSEUM OF SCOTTISH RAILWAYS

*+44 (0)1506 825855 *bkrailway.co.uk

Operated by the Scottish Railway Preservation Society. The railway has been developed since 1979 on reclaimed land and runs steam and heritage diesel trains from Bo'ness station, which opened in 1981, to Manuel, the terminus since 2013. The line had previously extended from Bo'ness to Kinneil (1984) and from Kinneil to Birkhill (1989).

A number of historic railway buildings have been acquired and reconstructed, and the Museum is Scotland's largest railway museum, home to a fascinating collection of locomotives, wagons and carriages, models, displays and photographs.

In the words of the Scottish Railway Preservation Society: 'Get hands on and discover railway history through fun interactive displays. Climb on board our vintage Glasgow Subway car and feel the past surround you. Become a signalman and pull the levers on the authentic signal-lever frame and challenge your friends to work out how to operate the points. Get an insight into life aboard a travelling Post Office Coach by sorting the letters yourself and don't miss the famous video of the Night Mail.'

BO'NESS MOTOR MUSEUM

Bridgeness Rd, Bo'ness EH51 9JR *+44 (0)1506 827007
*bonessmotormuseum.co.uk

The Motor Museum is one of the Falkirk & Forth Valley's only 4-star rated visitor attractions, and has been welcoming car aficionados since April 2004. Some 25 vehicles and a large collection of memorabilia and props are on display, with an emphasis on fictional secret agent James Bond 007, as well as items relating to the Harry Potter and 51st State movies.

BLACKNESS CASTLE

Blackness, Linlithgow, West Lothian EH49 7NH *+44 (0)1506 834 807
*historicenvironment.scot

Located 4.2 miles east of Bo'ness via the B903. If Blackness Castle looks vaguely familiar, it may be because you are a fan of the

▲ *Blackness Castle*

TV series Outlander. Blackness stood in for Fort William in series one of the epic time-travelling saga.

The castle was built in the 15th century beside the Firth of Forth as a residence for the Crichtons, then one of Scotland's most powerful families, and passed to King James II in 1453, along with the Crichton estates. In 1537, King James V commenced work to transform Blackness into a major defensive artillery fortification and prison.

In its role as a state gaol, Blackness housed high-profile prisoners such as Cardinal David Beaton, Archbishop of St Andrews, and a rival to the Earl of Arran, who acted as Regent while Mary Queen of Scots was a child and was imprisoned here during 1543. Later, Blackness held soldiers and sailors captured during wars with France, Spain, and what was to become the United States of America.

In 1650 the mighty defences of Blackness Castle proved no match for the artillery of Oliver Cromwell, whose English forces had invaded Scotland, and the garrison was forced to surrender as a result. The damage inflicted on Blackness remains clear to this day.

In the late 19th century, Blackness Castle was used as an ammunition depot, and it saw service during the World War I in that capacity before being decommissioned and repurposed as a visitor attraction. From the seaward side, the castle looks remarkably like a grounded vessel, leading to its nickname as 'the ship that never sailed'.

▲ *Linlithgow Palace*

LINLITHGOW PALACE

✉ Linlithgow Palace, Kirkgate, Linlithgow, West Lothian EH49 7AL
☎ +44 (0)1506 842 896 ⊘ historicenvironment.scot

In the care of Historic Environment Scotland, 5.3 miles from
Polmont via A803.

The palace is located in the town of Linlithgow, which boasts
many ancient buildings, and is 20 miles from Edinburgh, via
the A90. Adjacent to the Palace is the 15th-century St Michael's
Church, topped by an eye-catching aluminium spire, representing
Christ's crown of thorns, added in 1964, while a plaque on the High
Street records the site of Scotland's first petrol pump, installed
in 1919.

The palace is quadrangular in design, with its four ranges
of buildings grouped around a central courtyard. According to
Historic Environment Scotland, 'at Linlithgow Palace the visitor
can step inside the ruins of Mary Queen of Scots' birthplace, gain
unique insights into the domestic life of Scottish royalty, see
the ornate fountain [dating from 1538] in action every Sunday in

July and August, admire elegant architecture such as the oriel windows of the king's and queen's bedchambers, enjoy open views from Queen Margaret's Bower over the peel and loch to the Forth bridges, have a picnic by the loch and spot some local wildlife, and take our fun fact-finding quiz while exploring the palace'. The name Linlithgow means 'the loch in the damp hollow' and the palace stands on a modest hill overlooking a small loch, which is notable for its wildfowl population. The site was first utilised by the Romans, some 2,000 years ago, and it is thought that the earliest royal residence here was established during the reign of King David (1124–53), while the town itself began to develop from that period.

Construction of the current palace began in 1424 on the orders of King James I, with the Great Hall being the principal building, while royal apartments were added by King James IV between 1488 and 1513. The palace served as a stopping place for royalty when travelling between Edinburgh Castle and Stirling Castle (see p.34). It was the birthplace of James V (1512), Mary Queen of Scots (1542) and Princess Elizabeth (1596).

Mary Queen of Scots, otherwise known as Mary Stuart or

Mary I of Scotland, was just six days old when she became queen, following the death of her father. She married the Dauphin Francis, heir to the French throne in 1558, briefly becoming queen of France as well as Scotland, when Francis succeeded his father in 1559, though he died the following year.

Back in Britain, Mary's Catholic faith counted against her in what was now officially a Protestant country, though she ruled Scotland until 1567. In that year Protestant nobles rose up against her, leading her to abdicate in favour of her son, James, whose father was Mary's second husband, David, Lord Darnley. Darnley was murdered in 1567, and Mary married the man widely believed to be the murderer, the Earl of Bothwell, just three months later. Mary was executed at Fotheringhay Castle in Northamptonshire on 8 February 1587, at the age of 44.

Once her son, King James VI, was crowned James I of England in 1603, the royal court moved to London and Linlithgow Palace fell into disrepair, with the 'north quarter' collapsing in 1607, though it was subsequently rebuilt on the orders of King James VI. However, a major fire in 1746 caused great damage to the palace, which was never again inhabited.

LINLITHGOW DISTILLERY

✉Unit 15, Little Mill Business Park, Mill Road Industrial Estate, Linlithgow EH49 7DA ✆+44 (0)1506 846873 🔗linlithgowdistillery.uk.

Linlithgow is a craft gin distillery, established by husband-and-wife team Ross and Alyson Jamieson, who decided to come out of retirement after selling their IT business and embark upon a new venture.

As they explain, 'There has been an influx of new gins on the market in the last five years and whilst most gins use a combination of similar botanicals, we needed to come up with something to make "LinGin" stand out. How will LinGin be different? Our local botanicals. This is what makes LinGin unique and that the recipe has been honed by our local tasters to give a truly community developed experience.'

As well as LinGin, a second gin, named Four Marys, is also produced. A cask-aged version of LinGin – which has spent time in a former single malt whisky barrel – is available in limited quantities from the distillery or its online shop.

The Jamiesons explain: 'We have two stills. Both are high tech and fully programmable and give us the ability to reclaim all the heads and tails from each distillation. Our 100L still is called Gleann Iucha (Gaelic for Linlithgow). Our 500L still is called Scotty after Montgomery Scott who will be born in Linlithgow in the year 2222. If you follow Star Trek you will know who he is.'

The distillery offers a 'Tour 'n' Tasting' experience. 'Join us for a tour of our craft distillery and learn how we make LinGin and the Four Marys,' say the Jamiesons. 'You will get to try all of our gins or if you are driving you can take your sample away with you to enjoy at home.'

FALKIRK

Falkirk, a large ill-built town, supported by the great fairs for black cattle from the Highlands, it being computed that 24,000 head are annually sold here. There is also a great deal of money got here by the carriage of goods, landed at Carron wharf, to Glasgow. Such is the increase in trade in this country, that about twenty years ago not three carts could be found in the town, and at present there are above a hundred that are supported by their intercourse with Glasgow.

Thomas Pennant, A Tour in Scotland, 1769 (London: Benjamin White, 1776)

The town of Falkirk (visitfalkirk.com) is situated in the Forth Valley, 23 miles north-west of Edinburgh and 20.5 miles north-east of Glasgow. During the Industrial Revolution of the 18th and 19th centuries, Falkirk grew to prominence as a centre for heavy industry, largely due to its location at the junction of the Forth & Clyde and Union canals, which provided vital transport links.

Iron and steel manufacture were at the heart of Falkirk's prosperity, with the Carron Company being established in 1759 and subsequently growing into one of the world's largest ironworks. The firm produced armaments for the army and Royal Navy, and later went on to make the classic British red letterboxes still in use today, as well as the iconic red phone boxes designed by Sir Giles Gilbert Scott.

The Carron Works closed in 2016, and only a sadly-neglected clock-tower (on Stenhouse Rd, FK2 8DR) remains in situ to remind visitors of what was once a world-leading company. Nonetheless, there are many positive reminders of the past around Falkirk which can be visited and explored.

WADE & TELFORD

"Between 1725 and 1737, Wade oversaw the construction of 250 miles of road and 40 bridges. These were built by labouring gangs, military engineers and estates staff. Where previously there had only been single tracks, proper roads soon appeared linking Perth, Inverness, Stirling, Fort William and Fort Augustus."

VISIT www.historicenvironment.scot

Craigellachie Bridge was designed by the renowned civil engineer Thomas Telford and built between 1812–1814.

Several important modern routes through the Highlands have their origins in the road-building programme undertaken at the behest of Major General George Wade during the first half of the 18th century, with the A9 between Dunkeld and Inverness being a prime example.

Wade's work was carried out following the Jacobite Risings of 1689, 1715 and 1719 which attempted to restore the Catholic King James VII and II to the throne of Scotland. In 1724, King George I sent Wade to Scotland to see what might be done to make the Highlands more secure.

Wade subsequently recommended the construction of a series of roads, bridges and barracks that would mean government troops could be moved quickly and efficiently to deal with any future outbreaks of rebellion.

MILITARY ROADS

"These roads, by rendering the highlands accessible, contributed much to their present improvement, and were owing to the industry of our soldiery; they were begun in 1723, under the directions of Gen. Wade, who, like another Hannibal , forced his way through rocks supposed to have been unconquerable: many of them hang over the mighty lakes of the country, and formerly afforded no other road to the natives than the paths of sheep or goats, where even the Highlander crawled with difficulty, and kept himself from tumbling into the far-subjacent water by clinging to the plants and bushes of the rock.

Many of these rocks were too hard to yield to the pick-axe, and the miner was obliged to subdue their obstinacy with gunpowder, and often in places where nature had denied him footing, and where he was forced to begin his labours, suspended from above by ropes on the face of the horrible precipice. The bogs and moors had likewise their difficulties to overcome; but all were at length constrained to yield to the perseverance of our troops.

"In some places, I observed, that, after the manner of the Romans they left engraven on the rocks the names of the regiment each party belonged to, who were employed in these works; nor were they less worthy of being immortalised than the Vexillatio's of the Roman legions; for civilisation was the consequence of the labors of both.

"These roads begin at Dunkeld, are carried

21

The Wade Bridge at Aberfeldy was built in 1733-34 over the River Tay, under the supervision of Lieutenant General George Wade

on thro' the noted pass of Killicrankie, by Blair, to Dalnacardoch, Dalwhinie, and over the Coryarich, to Fort Augustus. A branch extends from thence Eastward to Inverness, and another Westward, over High-bridge, to Fort William. From the last, by Kinloch-Leven , over the Black Mountain , by the King's house, to Tyendrum; and from thence, by Glen-Urqhie, to Inveraray , and so along the beautiful boundaries of Loch-Lomond, to its extremity.

"Another road begins near Crief, passes by Aberfeldy , crosses the Tay at Tay-bridge, and unites with the other road at Dalnacardoch; and from Dalwhinie a branch passes through Badenoch to Inverness."
Thomas Pennant, A Tour in Scotland 1769 (London: Benjamin White, 1776)

Although the term 'Wade's Roads' is applied to the project, much of the later construction was led by Major William Caulfeild, who carried on Wade's task after the first phase

had been completed. That initial phase included the strategically very important creation of Ruthven Barracks near Kingussie in 1721. From 1732, Inspector of Roads Major Caulfeild was responsible for developing a further 800 miles of road and many more bridges.

"General Wade's roads and bridges played an important role in imposing the Hanoverian government's authority in Scotland," according to historicenvirnoment.scot, "but they also opened up routes for trade, travel and tourism...

"By the late 18th century some of the steeper and more remote sections of the military road network had been abandoned. Other sections were incorporated into the civilian road network as it was improved and expanded through the nineteenth century."

Much of that programme of improvement and expansion came courtesy of the next influential figure to address the issue of the

thoroughfares of the Highlands, Scottish civil engineer Thomas Telford (1757-1834).

In 1802, Telford was engaged by the government to report on the state of Highland roads and other aspects of infrastructure, much of which had fallen into a state of disrepair. As a result of Telford's report, the Highland Roads & Bridges Commission and the Caledonian Canal Commission were established the following year.

Under the direction of Thomas Telford, the Highland Roads & Bridges Commission was responsible for the building of new roads and the maintenance of earlier military routes, and between 1803 and 1821 Telford oversaw the construction of 920 miles of road and more than 1,200 bridges in the Highlands, not to mention ferries and harbours. When it opened in 1822, the Caledonian Canal facilitated transport north and west of the Great Glen. Road construction was

supervised by John Mitchell (1779-1824), described by Telford as "...a man of inflexible integrity, a fearless temper and indefatigable frame."

The building of new roads ended in 1828, and the commissioners of the Highland Roads & Bridges Commission reported that when their work commenced, the Highlands had been "...barren and uncultivated ... and inhabited by poor and ill-employed peasantry," whereas when their work was complete, they had left the area "...with "a profitable agriculture, a thriving population, and an active industry."

Road maintenance was subsequently carried out by the Repair Commission until 1863, initially under the superintendence of Joseph Mitchell, son of John, with Joseph later taking on the role of engineer.

CALLENDAR HOUSE

Callendar Park, Falkirk FK1 1YR   +44 (0)1324 503770
falkirkcommunitytrust.org

Although you would be forgiven for not realising it, at the heart of Callendar House is a 14th-century tower house, with the present French Renaissance château Scottish baronial fusion dating from a reconstruction project of 1877.

The mansion is set in the 170-acre Callendar Park, which contains a section of the Antonine Wall, and the house itself has played host to such famous figures as Mary Queen of Scots, Oliver Cromwell and Prince Charles Edward Stuart in its time.

In 1963 Callendar House and some parkland were acquired by Falkirk Burgh Council, and since 2011 it has operated under the auspices of Falkirk Community Trust. As a major centre for local heritage, the house boasts exhibitions about its own history, the story of the Antonine Wall, and Falkirk's role in the development of the Industrial Revolution.

Visitors can also explore the restored 1825 kitchen, where costumed interpreters explain what life was like in a large household during the early 19th century, complete with samples of food from the period. There are also a series of galleries where artworks are displayed, plus a tea room and gift shop. The parkland is home to an arboretum, ornamental gardens, a family mausoleum, nine-hole golf course, and children's play park.

THE TWO BATTLES OF FALKIRK

22 July 1298

Having tasted victory against the English army of King Edward I at the Battle of Stirling Bridge (see p.39) on 11 September 1297 during the First War of Scottish Independence, the Scottish forces led by William Wallace – then Guardian of Scotland – were faced by a large, powerful English army in Scotland the following summer. Edward's forces included around 2,500 mounted knights and 12,500 infantrymen, with many of the infantry soldiers being experienced longbow men, while Wallace's forces comprised some 5,000 infantrymen and 1,000 mounted knights.

Wallace was forced to fight on a site close to the River Carron, near Falkirk, on 22 July 1298, and the Scottish army was defeated with the loss of approximately one-third of its troops. Falkirk is credited as the first significant victory for the longbow in battle.

Wallace subsequently fled north, burning Stirling (see p.33) and Perth (see p.55), and resigned his Guardianship of Scotland, as his reputation as a military leader had been severely damaged. He continued a campaign of guerrilla warfare against the English before being captured near Glasgow in 1305 and executed in London for treason on 23 August of that year.

The Battle of Falkirk and the role played by Wallace in the cause of Scottish independence is commemorated by the Wallacestone Memorial (Wallacestone Brae, FK2 0EE). This tall column surrounded by wrought iron railings was erected in August 1810. It bears the inscription: 'Erected to the memory of that celebrated Scottish hero Sir William Wallace'.

17 January 1746

Also known as the Battle of Falkirk Muir, this conflict took place on a moor (muir) to the south-west of Falkirk during the Jacobite rising of 1745/46. It came after the Jacobite army headed by Prince Charles Edward Stuart (Bonnie Prince Charlie) had decided not to continue its march on London, having reached Derby (130 miles from the English capital) on 4 December 1745. The decision was only taken after a great deal of heated argument, and without the knowledge that support for their cause was growing and there was a real sense of panic in London.

The Jacobites duly retreated into Scotland, laying siege to Stirling Castle (see p.34) in early January 1746. Troops of King George II, commanded by Lieutenant General Henry Hawley, were sent to break the siege, with Hawley staying at Callendar House (see above), while the Jacobite army was encamped to the west of Falkirk.

On the afternoon of 17 January, the Jacobites attacked Hawley's forces, which were not well prepared for battle, and with heavy snow falling and light fading, the forces of Charles Edward Stuart routed the left wing of Hawley's army, but the right wing stood firm. The Jacobites did not follow up their victory, however, allowing the government forces to retreat and regroup, and when the two armies met again at Culloden Moor (see p.122) in April, the Jacobite rising was ended by a crushing defeat.

The site of the battle is marked by a monument on Greenbank Rd (FK1 5PU), which was erected in 1927. An accompanying information board gives helpful context to the battle for the modern-day visitor. Tartan wreaths and scarves are often to be found at the monument, commemorating this Jacobite victory.

▲ *Rosebank distillery.*

ROSEBANK DISTILLERY

✉ Camelon Rd, Falkirk FK1 5JR ✆ +44 (0)1506 852205
🖰 rosebank.com. 1 mile west of Falkirk centre on the A803, at the junction with the A9 and B816.

Distillation recommenced in the summer of 2023 at the historic Rosebank distillery, which had ceased production in 1993. The distillery was founded in 1840, and is situated on the banks of the Forth & Clyde Canal. Ian Macleod Distillers purchased the site from Scottish Canals in 2017, also acquiring the Rosebank trademark and existing stocks of spirit from distilling giant Diageo.

A new 1,000-square-metre contemporary distillery with a production capacity of up to one million litres of alcohol per year has been created, and triple-distillation using three stills rather than the more common pair is practised, as was once traditional in the Scottish Lowlands. Rosebank's landmark chimney has been retained and historically significant canal-side buildings have been converted into a visitor centre, tasting room, shop and warehouse space. A range of tours is on offer.

Rosebank was often considered the finest of all Lowland single malt whiskies, and the revival of the distillery has been greeted with great pleasure by whisky fans around the world.

FALKIRK DISTILLERY

⌂ Grandsable Rd, Polmont, Falkirk FK2 0WA ✆ +44 (0)1324 281086
🖝 falkirkdistillery.com

Falkirk Distillery is located close to the A9 motorway and the
very start of the present A9 road. It is situated 28 miles from
Edinburgh and 23 miles from Glasgow, and is within an hour's
drive of 70 per cent of the Scottish population, so it is not
surprising that the visitor side of the operation is very important.
Wide walkways capable of accommodating wheelchairs are in
situ, along with a lift, and a spacious gift shop and 120-cover
restaurant adjoin the production area. Annual visitor numbers are
expected to be around the 80,000 mark.

The distillery is an imposing piece of traditional-style whisky-
making architecture, white-painted, with 'Falkirk Distillery
Company' emblasoned on the wall in time-honoured fashion, and
topped with twin copper pagodas. It is the brainchild of colourful
veteran local businessman George Stewart, who has an electrical
engineering background, and presides over successful electrical
and house-building companies. The distillery is very much a
family venture.

Initial planning permission was granted to build the distillery
on an 11-acre site on Grandsable Rd in Polmont during 2010, but
the project came up against issues relating to the proximity of
a section of the Antonine Wall. Archaeological investigations,
followed by the outbreak of Covid-19, meant that it was the
summer of 2020 before construction of the Stewarts' distillery

was completed and equipment installed ready to make spirit.

George Stewart's aim at the outset was to create a beautiful distillery building with some heritage, which is why he bought a pair of used stills and a mash tun from copper-smithing legends Forsyth of Rothes on Speyside. They had purchased the silent Caperdonich distillery that adjoined their premises and subsequently demolished it in 2010, salvaging all the equipment within.

The pair of Caperdonich stills acquired by Stewart are some 40 years old, and the copper-topped mash tun is of the traditional 'rake and plough' kind. Forsyth undertook the installation and also supplied a new mill, stainless-steel washbacks and all ancillary equipment. A 1958 Abercrombie spirit safe, purchased from Diageo, completes the pleasing mix of old and new that defines the production area.

Most of the Falkirk 'make' is being filled into first-fill Bourbon casks, along with some first-fill oloroso sherry casks, and the team intends to offer small-batch limited releases during the early days of the spirit's legal status as Scotch whisky from mid-2023 onwards. A general release of Falkirk single malt is unlikely to happen until the whisky is five years old.

ROUGH CASTLE EXPERIENCES

Rough Castle (FK1 4RS) is a Roman fort on the Antonine Wall, just over one mile south-east of Bonnybridge (4.7 miles west of Falkirk via A803). It is in the ownership of the National Trust for Scotland. ✆ +44 (0)1324 473206 🖱 roughcastleexperiences.co.uk

Rough Castle Experiences operate at Rough Castle. In their own words, they say that their work 'brings history to life, engages the local community and makes learning fun with exciting outdoor experiences and woodland events. When you walk in our woodland you walk in the footsteps of ancient Rome. Whether it is experiences such as archery and axe throwing on UNESCO world heritage site, the Antonine Wall, guided heritage tours on foot or by segway, Rough Castle Experiences will leave a lasting impression on customers of all ages, as they learn the history and heritage of the wonderful 80-acre site.'

Additionally, Rough Castle Experiences offer seasonal woodland events such as spectacular light shows and foraging expeditions.

SCHOOL OF WITCHCRAFT & POTIONS

✉47 High St, Falkirk FK1 1ES ✆+44 (0)1324 639676
🖱visitfalkirk.com

This is described as 'An immersive Wizarding World experience in the heart of Scotland. Enter into a world like you've never seen before. Meet our Potion Master and be immersed into the creation of potions, wand movements, spells & so much more!'
   The School is intended for the biggest fans of the wizarding world and features 'realistic and antique props, moving pictures, magical sounds & cauldrons'.

FALKIRK WHEEL

✉Lime Rd, Falkirk FK1 4RS ✆+44 (0)870 050 0208
🖱scottishcanals.co.uk

A visually spectacular piece of engineering, the Falkirk Wheel was the first boat lift to be constructed in Britain since 1875, and is the only rotating boat lift in the world. It links the Forth & Clyde and the Union canals, allowing uninterrupted navigation from the east to the west coasts of Scotland, and is operated by British Waterways. The Wheel is 115ft tall, and was officially opened by HM The Queen in May 2002, as part of the 'Millennium Link', which restored both the Forth & Clyde Canal (opened in 1790) and the Union Canal (opened in 1822).

▲ The Falkirk Wheel

Although originally vital arteries of trade, by the 20th century canals had largely fallen into disuse, and the series of locks connecting the two canals was dismantled in 1933. The Forth & Clyde Canal closed in 1962, and the mid-1970s saw the Union Canal 'landlocked' by obstructions at both ends. The aim of the 'Millennium Link' was to encourage use of the canals for leisure, and a vast programme of work was undertaken to restore the canals and their many locks, with the project costing a total of £84.5 million. The task even included raising the level of the M8 motorway in one place.

Originally, the two canal systems had been joined by a series of 11 locks, which raised the level of water by 115ft from the Forth & Clyde to the Union Canal. However, such a time-consuming mechanism – taking the best part of a day to navigate – was unlikely to appeal to modern leisure sailors, so the idea of the Falkirk Wheel came into being. Its construction accounted for no less than £17.5 million of the entire project budget.

Two locks, a tunnel and a concrete aqueduct connect the Union Canal to the upper caisson, or gondola, of the Wheel, from where boats are lowered to the Forth & Clyde Canal, or raised from the Forth & Clyde Canal as required. Visitors without their own vessels can enjoy 60min boat trips on the Wheel, and the site also offers a free visitor centre and a café, bike hire, bumper boats and water 'peddlers'.

There is also the #Wheel2Kelpies Selfie Trail for energetic visitors, which connects the Falkirk Wheel to another of the area's must-see constructions. Get a map at the visitor centre or download one in advance, taking your first selfie and sharing it at @scottishcanals #Wheel2Kelpies, before setting off along the 4-mile route. There are four more selfies to be captured before you arrive at your destination – The Kelpies.

THE HELIX AND THE KELPIES

⌂The Helix FK2 7ZT ✆+44 (0)1324 590600 ⊘thehelix.co.uk

The Kelpies are a pair of 100ft-tall sculptures of horse's heads, intended to represent the supernatural water horses of Celtic myth and legend, which were also supposedly able to take on human form. They are said to appear in rivers and lochs, so their home as the gateway to an extension of the Forth & Clyde Canal is highly appropriate.

The Kelpies are the work of sculptor Andy Scott, and are

▲ *The Helix and the Kelpies*

intended to serve as a celebration of working horses in Scotland, whether towing barges on canals, playing an essential role in farming before the era of mechanisation or in industrial settings such as coal mines. To create the sculpture, Scott made three miniature versions in his workshop and these were then scanned by laser so that steel fabricators could replicate them accurately at full size. They each weigh 300 tonnes, and were made from structural steel and 928 individual stainless-steel skin-plates.

The Kelpies were unveiled to the public in 2014, and are clearly visible to anyone travelling on the M9 motorway between Edinburgh and Dunblane, much as The Angel of the North is a landmark for travellers on the A1 in north-east England. They are probably seen to their best effect when it is dark, as they are illuminated in a variety of changing colours.

The magnificent sculptures are the centrepiece of 'The Helix' parkland, which was created as part of the Falkirk Greenscape project designed to transform 350 hectares of land between

31

Falkirk and Grangemouth into a network of leisure spaces. The Helix Park opened in September 2013, and offers an Adventure Zone playpark and Splash Play area for youngsters, while a visitor centre, plaza café, and a programme of varied events provide something for everyone, no matter their age.

BANNOCKBURN BATTLEFIELD

⌂Bannockburn Heritage Centre, Glasgow Rd, Whins of Milton, Stirling FK7 0LJ ✆+44 (0)1786 812664 ⌾nts.org.uk

Operated by the National Trust for Scotland (NTS), the Centre allows the visitor to 'stand shoulder to shoulder with Robert the Bruce on the site of his greatest victory'. Visitors are invited to immerse themselves in the experience of the battle by way of a digitally recreated version of the conflict, and discover more about the tactics of the two opposing monarchs whose actions changed the course of Scottish history forever.

The centre encourages visitors to 'follow in the footsteps of Robert the Bruce in our memorial park and see the spot where he raised his royal standard. The Battle of Bannockburn experience puts you at the heart of the action so you can discover more about this crucial event in Scottish history. Outside, the landscaping and parkland around the centre allow visitors to appreciate the battleground and restored commemorative monuments, including the iconic statue of Robert the Bruce by Pilkington Jackson, cast in shimmering bronze'.

The Battle of Bannockburn was the culmination of the first of two Wars of Scottish Independence between the kingdoms of England and Scotland, which lasted from 1296 to 1357. During the first war, Scottish forces were led by Robert I, widely known as Robert the Bruce, who was King of Scots from 1306 until his death in 1329.

Bannockburn came at a time when English forces north of the border were very much on the back foot, with the Scots having taken all the strongholds of the English army, led by King Edward II, with the exception of Stirling Castle (see p.34). The besieged English forces within the fortress agreed to surrender if they had not been relieved by 24 June, and King Edward II assembled 13,000 infantrymen, including a contingent of Welsh archers, and 3,000 cavalrymen with the intention of breaking the siege. Opposing Edward was a numerically smaller force under Robert the Bruce, comprising 7,000 infantrymen, many of whom were pike-men, and several hundred light horse troops.

The subsequent battle – fought some 3.5 miles south of Stirling city – lasted for two days and ended with the Scots routing the English army, with Edward being lucky to escape with his life. In total, 34 English barons and knights were killed, while thousands of foot soldiers were killed or captured. On the Scottish side, only two knights lost their lives, along with several hundred infantrymen.

Bannockburn was the last significant victory of the Scots against the English during the Middle Ages, and the battle is credited with introducing new tactics throughout Europe, whereby infantry forces, not cavalry, dominated. Scottish independence was finally realised in 1328, 14 years after Bannockburn, with the signing of the Treaty of Northamptonshire.

However, peace was not to last, and a second war began in 1332, with the invasion of Scotland by Edward Balliol and a number of Scottish noblemen who had been disinherited by Robert I. Scottish independence was only guaranteed once more, in 1357, with the Treaty of Berwick.

THE CITY OF STIRLING

Sterling [sic] and its castle, in respect of situation, is a miniature of Edinburgh; is placed on a ridged hill, or rock, rising out of a plain, having the castle at the upper end on a high precipitous rock. Within its walls was the palace of several of the Scotch Kings, a square building, ornamented on three sides with pillars resting on grotesque figures projecting from the wall, and on the top of each pillar is a statue, seemingly the work of fancy.
Thomas Pennant, A Tour in Scotland, 1769 (London: Benjamin White, 1776)

What is now the City of Stirling (⊘yourstirling.com) originally grew up around Stirling Castle, which still dominates the skyline. Its position as the crossing point closest to the mouth of the River Forth made the settlement strategically important for travellers between the north and south of Scotland, and historically also made it attractive to invaders.

Legend has it that during the 9th century, the howl of a wolf alerted the residents to a Danish invasion, giving the garrison just enough time to tackle the invading forces and drive them back into the sea. Appropriately, a wolf features on the city's coat of arms. Its location makes Stirling the 'gateway to the Highlands', and it has been described as the brooch that clasps together Highlands and Lowlands.

Stirling Castle

King David I designated Stirling a Royal burgh in 1130, and it was briefly the capital of Scotland, with King Robert the Bruce holding a parliament there in 1326. Today, Stirling's 'old town' boasts many historic buildings, and a range of information boards are very useful in providing context to places and events. Stirling was granted city status in 2002 as part of Queen Elizabeth II's Golden Jubilee celebration, and since 1967 it has been home to Stirling University, giving it a vibrancy and modernity to contrast with all those reminders of a proud and stirring past.

STIRLING CASTLE

Castle Esplanade, Stirling FK8 1EJ +44 (0)1786 450 000
stirlingcastle.scot

Visiting Stirling and its magnificent castle today, it is not difficult to see why the fortress was constructed there. It sits atop a volcanic rock, close to the River Forth. The castle was

established no later than the early 12th century, and most of the fortress as it stands was built between 1490 and 1600, with the three Stewart monarchs James IV, V and VI making it one of their key strongholds and residences. During the Wars of Scottish Independence (1328–57) the castle changed hands no fewer than eight times in half a century, and its strategic importance is reflected in the fact that the pivotal battles of Bannockburn (see p.32) and Stirling Bridge (see p.38) both took place within sight of its walls. In peacetime the castle was a centre of court life and government, and Mary Queen of Scots and James VI both counted it as home during their childhoods.

As a military stronghold, the castle ultimately became the regimental depot of one of the most famous regiments in British history, the Argyll & Sutherland Highlanders (now the 5th Battalion Royal Regiment of Scotland) from 1873 to 1964, though it remains the 'Argylls' spiritual home.

At the heart of the castle is the magnificent Great Hall,

a banqueting hall built to the orders of King James IV and completed in 1503. James VI held a great banquet in 1594 to celebrate the baptism of his son, Prince Henry, and the lavish nature of the event can be gauged by the fact that the fish course was served in a large wooden model ship, which even boasted real firing cannons! The Great Hall was restored in 1999 and externally rendered in distinctive Royal Gold colouring, which is how it would have appeared during the 16th century.

Another fascinating building at the heart of the castle is the Royal Palace, created for King James V (1512–42) and considered one of the best-preserved Renaissance buildings in Britain. A major restoration of the Palace was completed in 2011, and it is decorated and furnished as it would have been in the 1540s, when a young Mary Queen of Scots lived there. Costumed 'characters' are on hand to engage with visitors and tell tales of the Palace in its heyday.

A key feature of the Palace is The Stirling Heads Gallery, which houses a collection of 16th-century oak carved medallions, depicting monarchs, emperors, and classical mythological and Biblical figures. The Palace is also home to the Hunt of the Unicorn tapestry, a modern recreation of an early 15th-century design. It comprises seven individual tapestries that took 13 years to weave and cost £2 million.

Other sights to see in the castle include The Chapel Royal, built in 1593/4, the Great Kitchens, which give a lively insight into life 'below stairs', and the Palace Vaults, filled with fun interactive experiences, aimed at younger visitors. There is also an excellent museum devoted to the Argyll & Sutherland Highlanders. Additionally, the castle boasts a restaurant and three gift shops.

ARGYLL'S LODGINGS

🏠Castle Wynd, Stirling FK8 1EG ✎ +44 (0)1786 450000
🖉 historicenvironment.scot

Argyll's Lodgings are to be found close to the castle esplanade, and this mansion is said to be the most significant town house of its period to survive in Scotland. The Lodgings as it appears today was constructed around an existing 16th-century tower house during the 1630s for Sir William Alexander, 2nd Earl of Stirling. The 9th Earl of Argyll had the Lodgings extended during the 1670s, when it became his home, and during the Jacobite rising of 1745/46 the Duke of Cumberland – leader of the government forces – stayed in the Lodgings. In the early 19th century, the building served as a military hospital, later operating as a youth hostel. A major programme of restoration and redecoration allowed the Lodgings to open in its present guise during 1996. At the heart of the mansion are the splendid State Apartments, which show off the building as it would have been at its most opulent, when the Earl of Argyll was in residence.

OLD TOWN JAIL

St John St, Stirling FK8 1EA +44 (0)1786 464640 oldtownjail.co.uk

The Old Town jail opened in 1847 at a time when prison reform was an important social issue. It replaced the existing Tolbooth Jail, which was overcrowded and insanitary, and from 1888 until 1935 it served as Scotland's only military prison.

Restored during the 1990s, today the jail is a popular tourist attraction, where, as its website explains, you can discover 'tales of the horrible history of crime and punishment in the Royal Burgh of Stirling. You'll hear of infamous executioner Jock "The Happy Hangman" Rankin, along with murderers, martyrs and more. Our brand-new audio tour provides an intriguing (and safe) insight into the history of crime and punishment in Stirling'. An Escape Room experience is also on offer by prior arrangement, and there are panoramic views over the city landmarks and the Trossachs National Park beyond from the Observation Tower.

HOLY RUDE CHURCH

St John St, Stirling FK8 1ED +44 (0)1786 475275
holyrude.org

The Church of the Holy Rude – Holy Cross – stands close to the castle, and was established in 1129, making it the second-oldest surviving building in Stirling after the castle. It was the parish church of Stirling, but was destroyed by a major fire in March 1405, which decimated much of the settlement. However, rebuilding of the church began soon after, with the nave, South Aisle and Tower being completed around 1414. The oak-beamed roof of the nave is one of few surviving Scottish medieval timber roofs. More reconstruction occurred between 1507 and 1555, when a choir was added, extending the east end of the building, while the existing tower was increased in height.

King James VI (also King James I of England and Ireland from

1603) was crowned King of Scots in the church on 29 July 1567 by the Bishop of Orkney, and the Protestant leader John Knox preached a sermon to commemorate the occasion. The Church of the Holy Rude has the distinction of being the only church in Britain, apart from Westminster Abbey in London, to have staged a coronation and remains an active place of worship today.

STIRLING GIN DISTILLERY

The Old Smiddy, Lower Castlehill, Stirling FK8 1EN
+44 (0)1786 596496 stirlingdistillery.com

Cameron and June McCann established their distillery in 2019, producing gin in a historic building dating from 1888 situated within sight of Stirling Castle. The former blacksmith's workshop stands on the site where it is said King James V stabled his horses.

Stirling Gin and Battle Strength Gin are produced, along with the Folklore Collection of gin liqueurs. According to the McCanns, 'Our entire range is inspired by the mythologies and history surrounding Stirlingshire and its beautiful castle.'

Having established a range of bespoke whiskies sourced from third parties under the Sons of Scotland banner during 2020, the production of single malt whisky began in 2023. This was the first time that whisky had been distilled in Stirling since 1852

The Old Smiddy boasts a visitor centre and shop, and hosts Gin School sessions, where you can learn to make your own juniper-flavoured spirit, and there are regular distillery tours, tastings and masterclasses.

STIRLING OLD BRIDGE

The present Stirling Old Bridge – or 'Auld Brig' in Scots – is thought to date from the late 15th century, and provided a vital crossing point on the River Forth. Built of stone, it replaced its illustrious timber predecessor that was situated some 200yds upstream from the present structure and featured in the 1297 battle where an army led by William Wallace and Sir Andrew de Moray defeated the forces of King Edward I. Remains of the 13th-century timber bridge were discovered in 1990.

The bridge played a part in the Jacobite rising of 1745/46, when one arch was destroyed by government forces in order to frustrate and delay Prince Charles Edward Stuart and his troops as they marched south from the Highlands towards England.

BATTLE OF STIRLING BRIDGE

The battle took place on 11 September 1297, but had its origins in the death of the seven-year-old Queen Margaret of Scotland during 1290. This event left the throne of Scotland vacant, and the English King Edward I was keen to extend his power north of the border. Edward was given the chance to choose the next Scottish king, and opted for John Balliol, whom he believed would act as his puppet. However, Balliol proved to be much more his own man than Edward had anticipated, and in 1296 the English monarch invaded Scotland and deposed Balliol, going on to rule the country himself. At this point, the almost legendary figure of Sir William Wallace enters the story.

Wallace has been mythologised for centuries, most famously and controversially in the 1995 movie Braveheart, starring Mel Gibson as the Scottish hero, but the stirring nationalistic film certainly played fast and loose with historic facts.

Wallace's early life is not well documented, but it is known that he was born into a minor noble family, probably near Paisley, around 1270. His father was Sir Malcolm Wallace of Elderslie. As one of the leaders of resistance to King Edward I's actions in Scotland, William Wallace took up arms in 1296 and led a band of men who burnt the town of Lanark, killing its English sheriff, before turning their attention to Scone, near Perth, where the English king's representative was forced to flee.

Wallace and his followers proceeded to attack English garrisons between the rivers Tay and Forth, while fellow resistance leader and Scottish Steward Robert the Bruce was forced to surrender the army he had raised at Irvine. Undeterred by this, Wallace laid siege to Dundee before joining forces with Sir Andrew de Moray to face the large English army led by the Earl of Surrey, which was advancing on Stirling.

Wallace drew up his troops close to the Abbey Craig, just north of Stirling Bridge, and waited until the English army began to cross, two abreast due to the narrowness of the bridge. Once half the English troops had crossed the bridge, Wallace and his men attacked them from the higher ground where they were mustered, and the English knights struggled to handle the boggy ground of the riverbank, as well as facing the onslaught of Wallace's troops.

As a result, many of the English were trapped and killed, and others drowned, while the Earl of Surrey and those of his soldiers who had not yet attempted the river crossing fled the scene and

▲ *Stirling Old Bridge*

headed to Berwick. Some 5,000 of the 8,000–12,000 English and Welsh troops perished, while Sir Andrew de Moray suffered serious wounds and died eight weeks later.

The Battle of Stirling Bridge was a great success for the vastly outnumbered Scottish forces, and in its wake Wallace crossed the border and besieged Carlisle and burnt the Northumberland town of Alnwick. He returned to Scotland in December 1297 and was subsequently knighted and assumed the role of Guardian of Scotland (see Battle of Falkirk 1298, p.24).

NATIONAL WALLACE MONUMENT

🏠Abbey Craig, Hillfoots Rd, Stirling FK9 5LF ✆+44 (0)1786 472140
🔗nationalwallacemonument.com

Take the Wallace Way path from the Monument car park to the building itself, admiring the wood carvings along the way, or use the courtesy minibus as an alternative. Inside the Monument there is a well-stocked gift shop, which is the exclusive outlet for a limited-edition replica of Wallace's great sword, as well as a wide range of other gifts, including Scottish craft items, such as glassware, jewellery, pottery and clothing, along with children's games and toys. Additionally, an online shop provides another option to stock up on souvenirs.

The Monument houses three fascinating galleries, the first of which is the Hall of Arms. Here, the life of William Wallace is charted, as he rose to become leader of the Scots. An immersive animation illustrates his crucial role in the Wars of Scottish Independence, and star of the show is the Wallace Sword. This imposing weapon is a longsword, measuring 5ft 4ins long, and weighs 7lb. It was moved from Dumbarton Castle to the National Wallace Monument in 1889, having reputedly been at Dumbarton since 1305, when Wallace was imprisoned there. However, experts now believe that the sword actually dates from the 16th century.

The Hall of Heroes relates the stories of Scottish heroes from the time of Wallace to the present day, with the first bust – of Robert the Bruce – being placed there in 1886. Today 30 men and women are celebrated and honoured in this gallery.

The Royal Chamber is located on the third floor, and tells the story of the Battle of Stirling Bridge (see p.36), with weapons of the period on display and the chance to look out over the landscape as it is today, then compare it with the view Wallace would have had in 1297 courtesy of a detailed reconstruction of the area and its landmarks.

The Crown is the very top of the Wallace Monument – 246 steps from the ground floor – and provides stunning views across much of Central Scotland and even into the Highlands on a clear day.

The National Wallace Monument was the product of a competition to design a suitable memorial to William Wallace when Scottish national fervour was high in the Victorian era. The winner was Edinburgh-born, Glasgow-based architect J. T. Rochead, and the memorial was built between 1861 and 1869. It stands 67ft tall and is built from sandstone in Victorian Gothic style. It was paid for by public subscription and a number of private donations, including one from Giuseppe Garibaldi, a founder of modern Italy.

The idea of creating a memorial to Wallace had first been mooted almost half a century previously, with Glasgow being the intended site. However, the longstanding and enduring rivalry between the cities of Glasgow and Edinburgh meant that residents of the capital objected strongly to this plan. Ultimately, Stirling, approximately half-way between the two cities, was settled on!

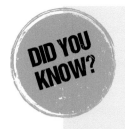

There are actually more than 20 Wallace monuments in Scotland, including Thomas Hamilton's Wallace Tower in Ayr (1833) and the Wallace Monument at Dryburgh (1814) in the Scottish Borders.

There is also a 30-feet high Wallace Monument on the west side of Druid Lake, Baltimore, in the US state of Maryland. According to baltimoreheritage.org, 'Beginning in 1905, the St. Andrew's Society of Baltimore, or the Scottish Society, has used the Wallace the Scot statue as a site of pilgrimage.

Gathering at the monument on St. Andrew's Day, the anniversary of real William Wallace's death, and the founding of their organisation in 1806, members of the society wear traditional clothing (such as kilts or capes) and celebrate their heritage as Scottish Americans'.

CAMBUSKENNETH ABBEY

Ladysneuk Rd, Cambuskenneth, Stirling FK9 5NG +44 (0)131 668 8600 historicenvironment.scot

The abbey is in the care of Historic Environment Scotland and is situated 1 mile east of Stirling, off the A907 road.

Cambuskenneth is regarded as one of the most important abbeys in Scotland, notable for its historic graveyard where James III and Margaret of Denmark were interred, along with many abbots. It is also renowned for its campanile, or bell tower, which dates from 1300 and was restored in 1864. The three-storey tower boasts a vaulted ground floor and pairs of lancet windows on each face of the belfry.

The abbey was established by King David I of Scotland in 1147, and was dedicated to the Virgin Mary. It was originally the Abbey of St Mary of Stirling, with the current name being adopted c.1207. It was significant because of its close proximity to the Royal Burgh of Stirling, which it served. In 1303 Robert Wishart, Bishop of Glasgow, swore an oath of allegiance to King Edward I of England at the abbey while, five years later, a number of leading

Scottish noblemen swore allegiance there to Robert the Bruce. After the Battle of Bannockburn in 1314 (see p.32) the abbey lands were used to share out the booty captured by Robert the Bruce and his army, and later the same year Bruce (King of Scots in 1306-29) held a parliament in the abbey.

In 1326, Cambuskenneth hosted another parliament, during which the clergy and nobility gathered to swear fealty to David Bruce, heir to Robert. Subsequently, King Robert II stayed at the abbey for some time and granted it charters, and his son, King Robert III, also visited in 1392, using it as a venue to conduct royal business. Following her death at Stirling Castle in 1486, Queen Margaret was buried at Cambuskenneth, followed two years later by her husband, King James III.

James perished in the aftermath of the Battle of Sauchieburn, fought on 11 June 1488 just south of Stirling between the king and a force of disaffected Scottish nobles. The Protestant Reformation of the 15th century, when the prevailing Catholic orthodoxy in Europe was challenged and Britain became officially a Protestant country, saw Cambuskenneth fall into disuse. Much of its masonry was subsequently removed and used as building material within Stirling Castle. The tomb of King James III was damaged during this time, but was restored during the 1860s, at the same time as the bell tower was renovated.

BLAIR DRUMMOND SAFARI PARK

⌂Blair Drummond Safari and Adventure Park, by Stirling FK9 4UR ✆+44 (0)1786 841456 ⬡blairdrummond.com. 6 miles north-west of Stirling via the A9 and A84.

Blair Drummond is home to more than 350 animals and offers an array of attractions sure to keep the whole family entertained. Highlights include:

- Safari Drive-Thru. Drive through various animal reserves in your own vehicle, getting the chance to observe wild and exotic animals from across the world, including lions, camels, antelope, rhinos, Barbary macaques and a pride of lions, not to mention monkeys in the Park's famous macaque drive-thru.
- Foot Safari. This is one of the best ways to get really close to some of Blair Drummond's most exotic creatures, with raised viewing platforms allowing visitors to observe lions, tigers and giraffes, along with access to the Elephant

▲ *A Barn Owl flying above Blair Drummond Safari Park.*

House, Rhino House and Lemur Land. Additionally, Pets' Farm is home to friendly horses, alpacas and sheep.

- A short boat trip takes you to Chimp Island, while for lovers of aquatic life, there are regular sea lion shows, and the sea lions may also be viewed in their outdoor pool. Additionally, bird of prey displays are staged at various times each day, providing great photo opportunities.
- World of Dinosaurs is entered through vast Jurassic Park-style gates, which lead into a prehistoric forest populated by more than 20 loud, life-size, moving dinosaurs.

As if that isn't enough, the Park boasts an adventure play area, complete with pirate ship and giant play fort, and there is also a range of amusement rides, including the Astroglide Slide and Flying Fox. And if all that activity leaves you hungry and thirsty there is a spacious restaurant and the Chakula Café. The gift shop offers a wide variety of souvenirs, and if you've been really inspired by your visit, you can even adopt one of the animals!

Blair Drummond Safari Park covers 160 acres and was established in 1970 with the assistance of Sir Jimmy Chipperfield, who had opened Longleat Safari Park in Wiltshire four years earlier. It is family-owned and run by Jamie Muir, who represents the third generation of his family to live at Blair Drummond. According to the Park's website, 'We're part of a worldwide network of zoos which cares for rare species, we are part of the Endangered Species Breeding Programme, and we support conservation projects in the UK and around the world.'

DOUNE

Situated eight miles north-west of Stirling via the A84, and some 3.5 miles beyond Blair Drummond.

The town of Doune was once renowned as a centre for the manufacture of fine flintlock pistols, with the Caddell family dominating the trade. No fewer than five Thomas Caddells made the distinctive ramshorn or scroll butt pistols between 1646 and 1776. It has been claimed that the first shot fired in the American War of Independence (1775–83) came from a Doune pistol.

Today, Doune is best-known for its medieval castle (Castle Hill, Doune FK16 6EA ✆+44 (0)1786 841742 ⌂historicenvironment. scot), once the seat of Robert Stewart, younger brother of King Robert III, 1st Duke of Albany and Governor of Scotland (c.1337–1406). The present castle dates from the late 14th century, though it is believed that an earlier fortification on the site had been built during the 13th century and suffered significant damage during the Wars of Scottish Independence.

Much of the castle is now in ruins, but in 1883 then owner the Earl of Moray ordered some restoration, and the Duke's Hall with its musicians' gallery, double fireplace and carved oak screen is a notable element of that restoration.

Doune castle is familiar to many people who have never visited, as it featured prominently in the 1975 film Monty Python and the Holy Grail, and more recently in Game of Thrones (as Winterfell) and Outlander (as Castle Leoch).

DEANSTON DISTILLERY

⌂Deanston, by Doune, Perthshire FK16 6AR ✆+44 (0)1786 843010 ⌂deanstonmalt.com

Deanston is one of those rare Scotch whisky distilleries to have been developed within an existing structure previously used for other commercial purposes. In Deanston's case that structure was the former Adelphi cotton mill, a listed 18th-century building beside the River Teith, a mile south-west of Doune.

Conversion work was carried out during the mid-1960s whisky 'boom' by the Deanston Distillery Company Ltd, formed by James

Finlay & Co and Tullibardine (see p.51) owner Brodie Hepburn Ltd. Deanston was purchased by Invergordon Distillers Ltd in 1972, first being bottled as a single malt two years later. However, the distillery closed in 1982, as the Scotch whisky industry reined in production, but was reopened in 1991, having been acquired by Burn Stewart Distillers for £2.1 million.

Deanston is a notably traditional distillery, despite its relatively modern origins, featuring a rare surviving open cast iron mash tun, and no computerisation of processes. It boasts the quirkiest maturation warehouse in Scotland, namely a vaulted ex-weaving shed, constructed in 1836, and was operating in an eco-friendly manner long before green became the new black, courtesy of a pair of water-driven turbines. Deanston distils from 100 per cent Scottish barley and was one of the first distilleries to make organic whisky, with regular batches being produced since 2000.

The house style is fragrant, medium bodied, malty and nutty. Virgin Oak, 12-Year-Old and 18-Year-Old are the principal bottlings available. The distillery shop stocks the definitive line-up of

▲ *Deanston Distillery on the River Teith*

Deanston single malts, including bottlings exclusive to the site, while tours of this most characterful distillery are regularly available.

ALLANWATER BREWHOUSE

Queens La, Bridge of Allan FK9 4NY +44 (0)1786 834555
allanwaterbrewhouse.co.uk

Bridge of Allan is an attractive Victorian spa town, 3.5 miles north of Stirling on the A9, and Allanwater Brewhouse is a great place to visit if you enjoy a pint or two of craft ale, or if you simply enjoy the atmosphere of a friendly pub environment.

- For those wishing to get up close and personal with the brewery, there are three tour options:
- The Bronze Tour offers participants the chance to discover how the raw materials of brewing are turned into beer, and also how the Brewhouse's Farmhouse Cider is made. Samples across the range of cask-conditioned and keg beers are on offer, along with a pint of your favourite beer or cider at the end of the tour.
- The Silver Tour involves a more in-depth exploration of brewing and cider-making, along with samples of beers and cider, a pint of beer or cider of your choice and homemade soup and sandwiches.
- The Gold Tour embraces all aspects of the Bronze and Silver, but concludes with a meal of homemade steak and kidney pie. Vegetarian options are available.

If you want to get personally involved in the brewing process there is a 'Brewer for a Day' option, which lasts approximately 4hrs and which the brewery describes thus: 'Spend a full day immersed in the traditional brewing process with our Head Brewer. Help with the mash and then relax with a light breakfast while planning the rest of the brew day. A very detailed, in-depth talk of the Brewing Process followed by hands on working (if desired). Take home to enjoy at your leisure the beer you have brewed with us at the brewhouse, either 20 litres draught pack or 24 x bottle conditioned Allanwater beers or ciders.'

The brewing experience is followed by a meal of homemade

soup and steak and ale pie, plus the opportunity to try a variety of bottled beers, and participants are presented with a framed certificate and photographs as mementos of the day. A 'Half Day Brewer for a Day' option is also available.

Whether or not you take part in a tour or brewing experience, the Brewhouse bar is a friendly, hospitable place to relax over a glass of something, offering the distinctive aroma of hops as you enter, seats by a wood-burning stove, and a bewildering array of bottled beers from all over the world. Eight beers and two ciders are always available on draught, there are board games and books, and regular music and quiz nights are staged, along with beer festivals.

The brewery was established in 1996 by local businessman Douglas Ross, and around a dozen different beers are available in bottle, ranging from the light, refreshing Lomond Gold up to the substantial Porridge Oat Stout, while some 30 cask ales are brewed.

As an Allanwater spokesperson explains, 'From the more traditional brews such as 70/- and Pot Black Stout to the experimental and eclectic such as Thai Pot and Chilli, Douglas and his brewers are always up for the challenge of cultivating new recipes whilst maintaining the excellence of the old ones. All the while they stand firmly by their ethos of only using the most natural as well as ethical ingredients and processes.'

DUNBLANE

Dunblane is located six miles north of Stirling and boasts a heritage dating back to 602, when it is said to have been founded by Celtic missionary St Blane at a crossing point on the Allan Water. There was probably a religious centre there from the 9th century, and the settlement grew in stature after the construction of its cathedral from the 12th century onwards.

The earliest surviving element of the original Dunblane Cathedral (⌂ The Cross, Dunblane, Perthshire FK15 0AQ ✆ +44 (0)1786 825388 🕾 dunblanecathedral.org.uk) is its red sandstone tower, but as late as 1237 the main cathedral was still without a roof, and in that year Bishop Clement was given permission by the Pope to create a new, larger cathedral on the site.

This structure fell into disrepair after the Protestant Reformation, with only the chancel being used for worship, and the roof of the nave collapsed in 1622. The chancel was restored in 1812, but by the 1880s it was considered too small to accommodate congregations. Accordingly, from 1889 the nave was restored in Gothic style by Sir Rowand Anderson. Venture into the cathedral today and the medieval stone walls of the nave that spent three centuries open to the elements remain rough and weathered, as testimony to the building's fluctuating fortunes through history. There are also notable Pictish carved stones and surviving 15th-century choir stalls in what is undoubtedly one of Scotland's finest medieval places of worship.

Sadly, the name of Dunblane often conjures up images of the horrific school massacre that took place there during 1996. A memorial to the 17 victims now stands in the south aisle of the cathedral.

Another must-visit building in Dunblane is the Leighton Library (✉ The Cross, Dunblane FK15 0AQ ☎ +44 (0)1786 822034 🖰 leightonlibrary.org.uk), Scotland's oldest private library, established around the collection of Robert Leighton, Bishop of Dunblane from 1661 to 1670. The library is now home to some 4,500 books in 89 languages, and visitors are able to explore the literary treasures, including a first edition of Sir Walter Scott's 1810 narrative poem, The Lady of the Lake.

One of Scotland's greatest sportsmen, the tennis legend Sir Andy Murray grew up in Dunblane, and on the town's High Street is a post box which was painted gold to commemorate the first of his two Olympic gold medal victories in 2012.

Another remarkable Scot with strong Dunblane connections was World War II hero Colonel Sir David Stirling (1915–90), founder of the Special Air Service (SAS). Stirling was born into a military family at the ancestral estate of Park of Keir, and in 2002 a splendid bronze memorial was erected at Hill of Row, west of Dunblane via the B824 to Doune. It features the figure of Stirling standing on rocks, and bears a plaque which reads: 'In remembrance of all those members of the Special Air Service Regiment who have died in the service of their country and have given their lives to uphold the principles of freedom and justice.'

THE BATTLE OF SHERIFFMUIR

The battlefield is situated on the slopes of the Ochil Hills, just within the Perthshire border and 4 miles east of Dunblane (see above) via the A820 and B8033.

The Battle of Sheriffmuir – or Sherrif Muir – took place on 13 November 1715. It was fought between a government force comprising Scottish and English regiments led by the Duke of Argyll and a Jacobite army led by John Erskine, Earl of Mar, intent on returning James Francis Edward Stuart – the 'Old Pretender' – to the throne. Mar had raised the Jacobite standard at Braemar in Aberdeenshire on 27 August 1715, and the Battle of Sherrifmuir took place as he marched to capture Stirling Castle and was intercepted by Argyll's troops.

The Jacobite army outnumbered government soldiers by two to one, but the battle of Sherrifmuir was inconclusive, with

▲ Dunblane

both sides claiming victory, and Mar was forced to retreat to Perth. The rising ended the day after the battle of Sherrifmuir, when Jacobite commander Thomas Forster surrendered to government troops led by General Charles Wills at Preston in Lancashire after several days of fighting.

TULLIBARDINE DISTILLERY

Stirling St, Blackford, Auchterarder, Perthshire PH4 1QG +44 (0)1764 682252 tullibardine.com

There are two tour options on offer at Tullibardine: the Classic Tour lasts around 45mins and includes a tour of all the processes of whisky-making, concluding with two different drams of single malt in the Dramming Bar. The Bonded Tour provides a more in-depth 90mins experience, and provides the opportunity to nose whisky in the cask in one of the distillery

warehouses, followed by sampling three single malts in the Dramming Bar, one of which is a 20-year-old Tullibardine. Visitors leave with a complimentary Tullibardine gift bag.

The distillery traces its roots back to 1488, when King James IV stopped off on his way to his coronation at Scone (see p.65) near Perth to acquire beer from the local brewery. Such was the quality of the beer, thanks in part to excellent local water sources, that by 1503 James Whisky-making was taking place in the vicinity of the current distillery in 1798, when William and Henry Bannerman began to distil, although the operation failed after just one year. Andrew Bannerman had more success when he revived the distillery during 1814, as it ran until 1837. During the 19th century, the village of Blackford boasted three breweries and a malting plant, with the last brewery closing in 1927.

Distilling returned to the village in 1949, with the distillery you see today being designed by William Delmé-Evans, who went on to create the Isle of Jura and Glenallachie distilleries. It was operated by Brodie Hepburn Ltd from 1953 until the Glasgow whisky-broking firm was taken over by Invergordon Distillers Ltd in 1971. Tullibardine's capacity was subsequently increased by the installation of a second pair of stills in 1973, and when Invergordon was acquired by Whyte & Mackay Distillers Ltd during 1993, the Perthshire plant was considered surplus to requirements, closing the following year. Happily, for Tullibardine, however, a business consortium bought the site from Whyte &

▲ *Tullibardine Distillery*

Mackay Ltd for £1.1 million in 2003 and recommenced distilling, introducing visitor facilities at the same time. Today, Tullibardine is owned by the French family firm of Terroir Distillers, which has added more warehousing to the site, created an in-house bottling line, and fitted out a cooperage.

The house style of Tullibardine single malt is elegant, floral, fruity and malty, with a spicy edge. The principal bottlings of Tullibardine in the Signature Range are Sovereign, 225 Sauternes Cask Finish, 228 Burgundy Cask Finish, and 500 Sherry Cask Finish. A Tasting Collection Set, containing 4 x 50ml bottles, is a great way of getting to know more about these whiskies, while 15, 20 and 25-year-old bottlings are also available. For those with very deep pockets, limited editions of single malts dating back as far as 1952 have been released in the Custodians Collection.

AUCHTERARDER

Auchterarder is often known as 'the lang toun' or 'long town' on account of its 1.5 mile-long High Street. In medieval times it was of strategic importance, but gradually declined, as Crieff, some 10 miles to the north-west, grew in stature. After the indecisive Battle of Sheriffmuir (see p.50) was fought nearby in November 1715, the Jacobite forces led by the Earl of Mar burnt Auchterarder to the ground.

The town's fortunes improved after the Perth to Stirling

railway line opened in 1848, providing Auchterarder with a mainline station. This station was to be important to the town's future prosperity as the Caledonian Railway Company began to construct a luxury country house hotel and golf course west of Auchterarder, at Gleneagles.

GLENEAGLES

⌂ Auchterarder PH3 1NF ✎ +44 (0)1764 662231 ⏱ gleneagles.com

Gleneagles is a five-star hotel, spa and golf resort less than three miles from Auchterarder via the A824. When it opened its doors in 1924 it earned the plaudit 'A Riviera in the Highlands'. It even boasted its very own railway station, still in use today, though the Caledonian Railway had been taken over by London, Midland & Scottish Railway (LMS) by the time the hotel was completed.

As the present owners say, 'Take a look inside the Glorious Playground… A charming country estate, a rural family adventure, a luxurious escape for friends, a cosy couples retreat, a home from home – Gleneagles is a luxury 5-star hotel like no other.'

All rooms and suites are individually designed and as stylish as you would expect, and there are no fewer than 10 different bars and restaurants, including the Andrew Fairlie, which remains Scotland's only two-Michelin-starred restaurant. Meanwhile, The Gleneagles Retail Arcade showcases luxury boutiques and brands more usually associated with London's West End than rural Perthshire.

Golf is still at the heart of Gleneagles, which is equipped with three championship courses, the most recent having been designed by golf legend Jack Nicklaus and opened in 1993. Originally named The Monarch's Course, it was subsequently renamed The PGA Centenary Course and was the venue for the 2014 Ryder Cup between Europe and the USA. There is also a 9-hole Academy course and nearby Dormy Club House, which offers changing rooms and saunas for golfers, a shop selling everything golf-related from Gleneagles polo shirts to golf clubs, and the Auchterarder 70 Bar with craft beers and sharing plates, plus the adjacent Blue Bar, an outdoor space for the enjoyment of fine whisky and cigars.

Apart from golf, Gleneagles boasts a wide range of other sports and leisure facilities, including an equestrian school, fly-fishing, shooting, falconry, tennis, croquet, off-road driving courses and archery. For a more chilled-out time there is a leisure club,

▲ *Gleneagles Hotel*

equipped with two indoor pools, a heated outdoor pool, jacuzzi and steam room, plus gym and fitness training facilities for when you feel the need to be more energetic. Perhaps most intriguing of all is the Gundog School at Gleneagles, where your dog can enjoy comparable comfort to its owner, in state-of-the-art kennels complete with soft mattresses!

PERTH

This town was unhappily for some time, the seat of the late rebellion [1715 Jacobite rising]; but I cannot say it was unhappy for the town: For the townsmen got so much money by both parties, that they are evidently enrich'd by it; and it appears not only by the particular families and persons in the town, but by their publick and private buildings which they have rais'd since that; as particularly a new Tolbooth or Town-hall.

Daniel Defoe, A Tour thro' the Whole Island of Great Britain, 1724

Perth (⏚ perthcity.co.uk) has long been known as 'The Fair City', having been granted what is known as the 'Golden Charter' by King James VI in 1600. In this document he described Perth as '...a free city and a regal and royal burgh'. Officialdom took away Perth's official city status in 1975 as part of local government reorganisation, but much to the delight of Perth residents it was restored in 2012, when Perth won a competition to become a city once more to mark the Queen's Diamond Jubilee.

This only seems fair when you consider how historically important Perth has been, effectively serving as the first capital of Scotland from the 800s until 1437. The first written record of the burgh dates from the early 12th century, by which time Perth was already a prosperous and thriving settlement. Its origins date back much further, however, as evidenced by the discovery of a prehistoric canoe near the present harbour which was dated to between 8,000 and 6,000 BC.

Perth's prominence was principally due to its location as the highest navigable and lowest fordable point of the mighty River Tay, Scotland's longest river at almost 117 miles. In 1922 Miss Georgina Ballantine caught a 64lb salmon on the Tay, a weight which is still a record for a British rod-caught salmon. As well as its strategic location by the Tay, Perth is also close to the ancient coronation site for Scottish monarchs at Scone (see p.65) and some 45 miles north of Edinburgh, giving it the status of one of the 'gateways to the Highlands', along with Stirling (see p.33), 34 miles to the south-west.

In times past, the city was home to royal courts and parliaments, was occupied by the forces of Oliver Cromwell in August 1651, and played host to both James Stuart, 'The old Pretender,' in January 1716 during the Jacobite rising of 1715/16, and his son 'The Young Pretender,' Charles Edward Stuart, in September 1745.

It also witnessed the murder of one monarch and the narrow escape of another. Of the many occasions when Perth was at the centre of Scottish life, two episodes stand out, the first being the murder of King James I in 1437 and the second being the sermon preached by John Knox in St John's Kirk during 1559, an event that sparked the reformation.

For many years, the now lost Blackfriars friary was pressed into service as a royal palace when members of the monarchy visited Perth. In February 1437 the court was based in the city for Christmas celebrations. On 21 February Robert Stewart of Atholl and Robert Graham led a force of 300 men intent on killing the autocratic King James. He was captured and slaughtered while trying to escape, via a privy, or toilet, if legend is to be believed.

In his St John's sermon of 11 May 1559, John Knox exhorted the congregation to 'purge the churches from idolatry'. Inflamed by his oratory, worshippers smashed the altars in St John's, before wrecking Loretto Chapel, St Ann's Chapel, and the monasteries of Greyfriars, Whitefriars, Blackfriars and Charterhouse. The present St John's Kirk dates from the 15th century and is Perth's only surviving medieval building.

There is an old joke to the effect that Perth was the smallest city in Scotland because it lies between two inches. The name 'Inch' derives from the Gaelic for small island, and the two low-lying areas of land known as the North Inch and South Inch have long been treasured green spaces for recreation in the city. In 1396 the North Inch was the location of a famous battle between representatives of the clans Chattan and Kay. A longstanding feud between the two clans was settled by armed combat between 30 men of each side, with the fight being witnessed by the king. 48 of the 60 men are said to have perished. A fictional account of the conflict forms the climax of Sir Walter Scott's novel, *The Fair Maid of Perth*.

Trades such as weaving and dyeing were at the core of Perth's prosperity from early times, and these and other industries expanded with the arrival of the railway in 1848. In particular, Perth grew into an important centre for whisky blending, being ideally suited to receive casks of single malt whisky from Highland distilleries by rail, blend them with grain whiskies and then transport them by train to the markets of the Lowlands and England. Local families such as Bell and Dewar became household names all over the world thanks to blended Scotch whisky.

Today, Perth offers a wide range of attractions that make a detour from the A9 bypass of the city – opened in 1978 – well worthwhile.

RSGS AT THE FAIR MAID'S HOUSE

North Port, Perth PH1 5LU ℘+44 (0)1738 455050 ℗rsgs.org

The Fair Maid's House dates in part from 1475. Sir Walter Scott portrayed Catherine Glover – the 'Fair Maid' – as living there in 1396, and in 1629 the influential Glovers' Incorporation of Perth acquired the house and used it as a meeting place for more than a century and a half. The property was renovated in 1893–94 and little of the medieval structure survives.

Today the house is home to The Royal Scottish Geographical Society, an educational charity, and a visitor centre showcases the work the Society does and its historical collections. As the Society explains, 'The RSGS Fair Maid's House Visitor and

▲ *Perth and the River Tay art trail*

Education Centre is a geographical delight housed in the oldest secular building in Perth. Visitors can watch the planet from space in the Earth Room, see the continents evolve and learn about the hottest and coldest places on Earth in the Education Room, and learn about maps and explorers, or curl up with a book, in the Explorer's Room.'

The Fair Maid of Perth is also commemorated as a bronze statue of Catherine Glover by Graham Ibbeson. The statue is located on Perth High St and features Catherine seated on a bench with a book in her lap.

PERTH MUSEUM & ART GALLERY

⌂78 George St, Perth PH1 5LB ✎+44 (0)1738 632488
⌖culturepk.org.uk

The Museum & Art Gallery is a striking building with external columns and a copper domed roof, its architectural style belying the fact that it was only constructed in the 1930s. Inside, the permanent collection is a treasure-trove of items relating to the

city and the county of Perthshire, with local history the focus of the 'Beginnings Gallery', while 'Wild and Wonderful' explores the natural history of the area. There is also a range of artworks on display.

Perth and Kinross Council states: 'From portraits and photographs to meteorites and Miss Ballantine's salmon, this fascinating array of objects will amaze young and old alike – do look ahead of visiting to find out about the in-gallery activities for families.'

FERGUSSON GALLERY

Marshall Pl, Perth PH2 8NS + 44 (0)1738 783425, culturepk.org.uk

The Gallery celebrates the work of artist John Duncan Fergusson (1874-1961) and his wife Margaret Morris, a renowned dancer. In the words of Perth & Kinross Council: 'Born in Edinburgh, with ancestral links to Perthshire, Fergusson spent much of his career in France and is now most associated with the Scottish Colourist group. The Fergusson Gallery holds his vast collection of artwork and associated archive, along with the archive of his lifelong companion, the pioneer of modern dance, Margaret Morris.'

The Gallery is housed in a remarkable building which started life as Perth waterworks. It was designed in 1830 to supply water to houses in the city for the first time, and was one of the earliest buildings in the world to be constructed from cast iron. It contained a tank that could hold up to 146,000 gallons of water and was operational for 133 years. The building subsequently served as a tourist information office before becoming home to the Fergusson Gallery in 1992.

PERTH DISTILLERY COMPANY

✉George Inn Ln, Tay St, Perth PH1 5LD ✆+44 (0)1738 638337
🖱perthdistillery.co.uk

The first distillery in Perth since the Isla whisky distillery at Bridgend fell silent in 1926 opened in November 2019. The Perth Distillery Company had been established by Iain McDonald three years earlier, with its gin originally being produced by a third party prior to a move to a labyrinth of rooms beneath the Royal George Hotel, located beside the River Tay in the centre of the city.

The distillery is equipped with two Portuguese alembic copper stills and produces a classic London dry gin-style of spirit using 15 botanicals. A pink gin – named Perth Pink – is also made, using Perthshire-grown raspberries. Distilling and bottling takes place on site, and members of the public are welcome to take the Classic Gin Tour or participate in the Perth Distillery Gin School.

THE RIVER TAY PUBLIC ART TRAIL

✉Riverside, Perth PH2 7TR.

The Norrie Miller Walk – named after civic leader Sir Francis Norrie Miller – is situated in Norrie Miller Park on the west bank of the River Tay, via South St. The Walk is home to a spectacular public art trail. Perth & Kinross Council explains: 'Featuring a variety of sculptures from artists including Tim Shutter, David Wilson, John Creed, Paul Eugene Riley, Kenny Munro, Doug Cocker and Phil Johnson, the art trail is themed around some of the most notable achievements of the city and its people.'

▲ *Black Watch Castle and Museum*

BLACK WATCH CASTLE & MUSEUM
⌂Hay St, Perth PH1 5HR ✆+44 (0)1738 638152 ⊘theblackwatch.co.uk

This five-star visitor attraction is dedicated to one of the most famous regiments in Scottish history, the Black Watch, which had Perth at the heart of its recruiting area. The regiment was formed in 1739, principally to defend against a Jacobite rising. Subsequently, it fought in virtually every action where British troop were engaged, including the Battle of Waterloo, the Crimean War, the Indian Mutiny, the Boer War, the First and Second World Wars, Korea, Kenya, Cyprus, Northern Ireland, Iraq and Afghanistan.

World War I was notably costly for the regiment, with 8,000 members lost and a further 200,000 wounded. Prior to the First World War, the Black Watch had earned 28 battle honours, and by the time the war ended it had gained a further 68, including four Victoria Crosses.

The museum is housed in Balhousie Castle, formerly a residence of the Earls of Kinnoull, which was built during the early 15th century, though the present structure largely dates from a restoration of 1864. It served as the regimental HQ from 1962 until the regiment was absorbed into the new Royal Regiment of Scotland, where it became the 3rd Battalion.

The Museum boasts an extremely attractive café which serves home-baking, and a well-equipped gift shop, stocking beauty products, jewellery and artisan food and drink from local suppliers, as well as children's gifts, toys, and Black Watch Regimental clothing and accessories.

WILLOWGATE ACTIVITY CENTRE

⌂Stockgreen Lodge, Lairwell, Perth PH2 7JU ✏+44 (0) 1738 637245 ⬀willowgateactivitycentre.co.uk

For a real outdoors experience, Willowgate offers activities such as target and combat archery, guided hill walks, bush craft, stand-up paddle boarding and open-water swimming. The Centre bills itself as 'Perthshire's Premier Outdoors Centre'.

Guided kayak tours of the Perth Loop on the River Tay are a popular option with visitors or, if you fancy being a bit more adventurous, choose the Perth to Fife Tour, which lasts for 3hrs and takes you all the way to Newburgh in Fife. Alternatively, a variety of pleasure cruise options on the Tay are available if you don't fancy getting your feet wet.

BRANKLYN GARDEN

⌂116 Dundee Rd, Perth PH2 7BB ✏+44 (0)1738 625535 ⬀nts.org.uk

Branklyn Garden covers two acres of hillside and are in the care of the National Trust for Scotland (NTS). They were created during the early 1920s by John and Dorothy Renton, alongside their splendid Arts and Crafts Movement-inspired house, located on the side of Kinnoull Hill.

According to the NTS, 'the couple were keen to have a garden that featured rare and unusual plants and flowers from all over the world. Thanks to the seeds collected by renowned plant hunters (including George Forrest and Frank Ludlow) and due to Dorothy's remarkable gardening skills, the couple's wish was granted. Today, gardeners and botanists come from across the globe to admire Branklyn's outstanding collection, particularly the rhododendrons, alpines and peat-garden plants. It also holds several National Collections of plants, including Meconopsis and Cassiope.'

After exploring Branklyn, visitors can relax over tea or coffee and home-baking on the terrace overlooking the garden.

HUNTINGTOWER

Huntingtower, by Perth PH1 3JL +44 (0)1738 627231
historicenvironment.scot
Accessed via the A85 Crieff road, 3 miles west of Perth city centre.

The present Huntingtower castle principally comprises two stone towers, constructed in the 15th and 16th centuries, joined together by a central structure during the 17th century. It was built for the Ruthven family and was initially known as Ruthven Castle or the House of Ruthven. It played host to Mary Queen of Scots and her husband Lord Darnley in 1565, while they were in the midst of seeing off a rebellion by a force of Scottish nobles, and is most notable for its role as a prison for Mary's son, the young King James VI.

The 4th Lord Ruthven, also 1st Earl of Gowrie, along with other Protestant activists, kidnapped the monarch in 1582, hoping to influence events in their favour by holding him prisoner at Huntingtower. The kidnapping was known as the 'Raid of Ruthven'. After 10 months in captivity, King James managed to escape, and actually went on to forgive Ruthven.

However, a second kidnapping – or perhaps even an assassination – attempt by brothers Alexander and John Ruthven in 1600 at their Perth residence of Gowrie House saw both siblings killed by members of the king's retinue, and all the family estates, including Huntingtower, were subsequently forfeited. The very name of Ruthven was proscribed, and the king decreed that Ruthven Castle should now be called Huntingtower.

While exploring this historic building, today's visitors can admire the painted wooden ceiling dating from around 1540, and the painted plasterwork of a similar date on the first floor of the Eastern Tower. The ceiling is said to be the earliest surviving example of its type in Scotland.

ELCHO CASTLE

Rhynd, Perth PH2 8QQ +44 (0)1738 639998
historicenvironment.scot
Accessed via the A989 and Rhynd Road, 4 miles south-east of the city centre.

Elcho Castle stands close to the south bank of the River Tay, and is an intact, 16th-century mansion house, built around 1560

▲ *Scone Palace*

as a country retreat for the prominent Wemyss family, who owned estates in Fife which later spawned lucrative coal-mining activities. The heir to the Earl of Wemyss holds the title Lord Elcho. Remarkably, Elcho castle still belongs to the Wemyss family, although it has not been lived in for some two centuries, and the interior is roofed, containing portions of original decorated plasterwork.

The castle's orchard has been replanted with traditional varieties of apple, plum and pear trees to restore an element of its living past, and visitors can enjoy beautiful views from the battlements.

SCONE PALACE

✉Perth PH2 6BD ✆+44 (0)1738 552300 🖉scone-palace.co.uk. 3.5 miles north of Perth city centre via the A93 to Blairgowrie, close to the village of Scone.

According to its owners, 'There can be few places of interest in Scotland as historically potent as Scone Palace. When you visit the palace you are walking in the footsteps of Scotland's ancient founding fathers, both pagan and Christian. It was an important religious gathering place of the Picts, it was the site of an early Christian church and it housed the Stone of Destiny.'

Scone Palace has been the ancestral home of the Murray

family, Earls of Mansfield, for over 400 years, and the present red sandstone building in Gothic Revival style dates from the early years of the 19th century, when the 12th-century original and later editions were completely remodelled and extended.

Internally, the palace is a delight for lovers of paintings, fine furniture and objets d'art, and contains bed hangings created by Mary Queen of Scots when she was imprisoned in Loch Leven castle during 1567–68, and the desk at which Queen Marie Antoinette wrote letters in the days preceding her execution by guillotine in Paris in October 1793.

Visitors may also explore the State Rooms, where Queen Victoria stayed while en route to the Highlands during 1842, and reflect on the fact that during the Jacobite risings, both James, 'The Old Pretender,' and his son 'Bonnie Prince Charlie' spent time in the palace.

However, it is as the coronation venue for Scottish kings that Scone is most renowned. From Kenneth MacAlpin in the 9th century to King Charles II on 1 January 1651, all kings of Scotland were crowned on the Moot Hill, initially seated upon the Stone of Destiny, also known as the Stone of Scone, until King Edward I removed it to London in 1296. Famously, Robert the Bruce was crowned on the Moot Hill on 25 March 1306.

A replica of the Stone of Destiny is located on the Moot Hill, while the original may now be viewed in Edinburgh Castle, after its return to Scotland in July 1996. However, 2024 will see the stone moved from Edinburgh to a new home in Perth's new £26.5m museum at City Hall. Moot Hill is also home to a Presbyterian chapel, rendered in Gothic Revival style, like the palace, around 1804.

The palace grounds are well worth spending time in, being home to the Murray Star Maze, planted in 1991 and boasting 2,000 beech trees and over 875yds of paths. Originally, the village of Scone was located within the palace grounds; when rebuilding of the palace took place in the early 19th century the village was relocated 2 miles away and christened New Scone.

Another must-see in the grounds is the David Douglas Pinetum, filled with giant redwoods and fine examples of the fir tree to which Scone-born one-time Palace gardener, botanist and explorer David Douglas (1799-1834) gave his name. The David Douglas Pavilion – appropriately constructed from Douglas Fir – offers an excellent interpretation of the life and work of Douglas.

PERTH RACECOURSE

✉Scone Palace Park, Perth PH2 6BB ✎+44 (0)1738 55159 ⎙ perth-races. co.uk.3.5 miles north of the city centre and accessed off the A93 road to Blairgowrie.

Britain's most northerly racecourse opened in 1908 and is the successor to race meetings staged on Perth's North Inch since the early 17th century. National Hunt or 'jump' race meetings are held between April and September, with the highlight being the Perth Festival in late April. Despite its distance from the main racehorse training centres, Perth attracts leading runners, owners, trainers and jockeys from far afield to compete, partly due to attractive levels of prize money, and partly due to the highly convivial atmosphere for regulars and newcomers alike. The picturesque, right-handed, 10-furlong track by the River Tay is one of five horseracing venues in Scotland.

SECTION TWO
Perth to Inverness

Birnam and Dunkeld	70	Highland Folk Museum	103
Beatrix Potter Exhibition and Garden	70	Ruthven Barracks	105
Dunkeld Cathedral	71	Speyside Distillery	106
The Battle of Dunkeld	72	Highland Wildlife Park	107
The Little Houses	72	BREAK OUT: SCOTTISH WILDLIFE	108
Dunkeld House Tree Trail	73	Aviemore and Carrbridge	113
The Hermitage	73	Rothiemurchus	113
Loch of the Lowes	75	Glenmore Lodge	113
Aberfeldy	77	Glenmore Forest Park	115
Aberfeldy Distillery	79	Cairngorm Mountain Ski Area	115
Blair Athol Distillery	82	The Strathspey Railway	116
Pitlochry	83	The Snug	117
Pitlochry Dam Visitor Centre	84	Cairngorm Brewery	117
Pitlochry Festival Theatre	84	Aviemore Kart Raceway	118
Enchanted Forest	86	Landmark Forest Adventure Park	119
Edradour Distillery	88	Tomatin Distillery	121
Queen's View and Killiecrankie	89	Culloden Battlefield	122
Blair Atholl	92	Inverness and Loch Ness	123
Atholl Country Life Museum	92	Inverness Museum and Art Gallery	125
Water Mill and Tea Room	93	Inverness Castle	125
Wasted Degrees Brewing	93	Uile-Bheist Distillery	126
Blair Castle	94	Abertarff House	128
House of Bruar	97	Inverness Botanic Gardens	128
Clan Donnachaidh Centre,		Eden Court	129
the Falls of Bruar	98	Inverness Victorian Market	129
Dalwhinnie Distillery	100	BREAK OUT: CLANS & TARTANS	130
Newtonmore and Kingussie	102	The Northern Meeting	134
Clan Macpherson Museum	102	Inverness Highland Games	134

PERTH – PITLOCHRY – 27 MILES
PITLOCHRY TO AVIEMORE – 57 MILES
AVIEMORE TO INVERNESS – 30 MILES

TOTAL DISTANCE – 114 MILES

North of Perth, the A9 travels into what is unmistakably the Scottish Highlands, featuring mountains, lochs, glimpses of red deer and road signs in English and Gaelic. Places such as Pitlochry and Aviemore are long-established holiday destinations, with the latter catering particularly to winter sports enthusiasts. Winters can be harsh this far north, and the presence of several sets of 'snow gates' to close the A9 when necessary serve as a reminder of that fact. At the northernmost point of this section of the road stands the city of Inverness, 'the capital of the Highlands', a fascinating location in its own right and a convenient base for wider exploration.

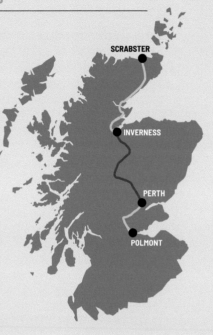

SCRABSTER

INVERNESS

PERTH

POLMONT

WHERE TO STAY

Hotels
Pitlochry
Fonab Castle Hotel
fonabcastlehotel.com
Knockendarroch Hotel
knockendarroch.co.uk
Kingussie
McInnes House Hotel
mcinneshousehotel.com
Aviemore
Cairngorm Hotel
cairngorm.com
Inverness
Kingsmills Hotel
kingsmillshotel.com

Caravan/Glamping/Campsites
Pitlochry area
Aberfeldy Caravan Park
aberfeldycaravanpark.co.uk
Aviemore area
Oakwood Caravan and Camping Park
oakwoodcampingpark.co.uk
Dalraddy Holiday Park
campinginaviemore.co.uk
Inverness area
Bunchrew Caravan Park
bunchrew-caravanpark.co.uk
Barrow Campsite
barrowcampsite.com

BIRNAM AND DUNKELD

dunkeldandbirnam.org.uk

North of Perth, the village of Birnam and the town of Dunkeld are located just to the east of the A9, some 14 miles from Perth, having been bypassed in 1977. The settlements are separated by the River Tay. Birnam is probably most famous for being referenced in Shakespeare's play Macbeth, where, in Act V, Scene III, Macbeth declares: 'I will not be afraid of death and bane, till Birnam forest come to Dunsinane.' The play mixes historical fact with dramatic fiction to great effect. Macbeth (c.1005–57) was a real king of Scotland, and Dunsinane Hill is a real place, located to the south-east of the village.

Another famous name connected with Birnam is Beatrix Potter, a writer more usually associated with the English Lake District. However, Potter's wealthy family spent summers during the salmon fishing season at Dalguise, 4.5 miles north of Birnam, and the young Beatrix came to love the natural world of the area, spending a great deal of time exploring and sketching. Her links to this part of Perthshire are celebrated in the attraction below.

BEATRIX POTTER EXHIBITION AND GARDEN

Station Rd, Birnam +44 (0)1350 727674 birnamarts.com

According to the dunkeldandbirnam.org.uk website, 'Children's activities at the Beatrix Potter Exhibition include dressing up to become Mrs Tiggy-Winkle, Peter Rabbit and Jeremy Fisher, or sit down and watch the enchanting stories unfold. Drawing, colouring, puzzles, rubbing panels featuring animal tracks and characters from the books, baskets of Beatrix Potter's much-loved books to look at. All recreating the Victorian world that Beatrix grew up in.'

Until the arrival of the Scottish Midland Junction Railway line in 1856, Birnam was a modest hamlet, but rail travel made the area accessible for tourism, and the village grew in scale as a result. It is linked to Dunkeld by a magnificent seven-arched stone bridge which spans the Tay, and was designed by the celebrated engineer Thomas Telford, opening in 1809. Until Birnam and Dunkeld were bypassed, this bridge was part of the A9, carrying increasing volumes of traffic as the 20th century progressed and tourism in the Highlands grew apace.

▲ *Beatrix Potter Garden.*

DUNKELD CATHEDRAL

⌂ Cathedral St, Dunkeld, Perthshire PH8 0AW
⏀ historicenvironment.scot

Dunkeld is best-known for its striking and beautifully situated cathedral ruins, located close to the River Tay. It is recorded that in 849 relics of St Columba were transferred from the island of Iona, where they were in danger from Viking raiding parties, to Dunkeld, on the orders of King Kenneth MacAlpin. A bishop of Dunkeld was appointed and Columba was declared the patron saint of Dunkeld and its monastery. The oldest surviving element of the cathedral is the choir, which dates from the late 13th century, while work on the nave started in 1406. The Protestant Reformation of 1560 saw the roof removed and deterioration of the remaining structures increased over time, as at so many religious institutions associated with the Catholic church.

Some 16th-century paintings survive on the vault of the ground floor in the bell tower, which was once an ecclesiastical court. The choir is home to the well-preserved tomb of Alexander Stewart, Earl of Buchan, son of King Robert II, widely known as 'The Wolf of Badenoch' and even as 'The Celtic Atilla' for his violent and destructive behaviour, which included the burning of the towns of Forres and Elgin, including Elgin cathedral, in 1390.

THE BATTLE OF DUNKELD

During the first Jacobite rising in 1689, government forces were defeated at Killiecrankie (see p.89) by the Jacobite army. The Cameronian regiment, commanded by Lieutenant Colonel William Cleland, was ordered to march north from Perth and hold Dunkeld against the Jacobites.

The Cameronians established defensive positions in the cathedral and the Marquess of Atholl's nearby mansion, managing to repel the subsequent Jacobite offensive, but they also came under attack from muskets deployed by Jacobite sympathisers in surrounding houses. The marks where musket balls struck the east gable of the cathedral can still be seen today. The Cameronians' response was to fire the thatches of every dwelling in the town, with the exception of three in which their own troops were located. Many Jacobites burned to death in the ensuing conflagration.

The battle lasted for 16 hours, with the Cameronians – outnumbered four to one – running out of ammunition, but at 11pm the Jacobites found themselves in the same situation and withdrew, having suffered casualties that numbered 300 dead or wounded. On the government side, William Cleland was mortally wounded during the first hour of the battle and lies buried in the cathedral nave, under a stone which bears nothing but his name.

THE LITTLE HOUSES

⌂Cathedral St & The Cross, Dunkeld PH8 0AN ⬦nts.org.uk.
The town of Dunkeld is small, and has a small linnen [sic] manufacture. Much company resorts here, in the summer months, for the benefit of drinking goats' milk and whey: I was informed here, that those animals will eat serpents.
Thomas Pennant, A Tour in Scotland, 1769 (London: Benjamin White, 1776)

Much of the historic centre of Dunkeld that exists today was constructed after the Battle of Dunkeld, and a notable feature are the 18th-century merchant dwellings, and smaller properties, concentrated around The Cross and in Cathedral St. Their survival is due to a collaboration between the former Perth County Council and the National Trust for Scotland, which set out in 1950 to restore existing buildings and fill gap sites with new structures that were in keeping with their surroundings. The restored properties were subsequently let to local tenants, having been gifted to the NTS by the Duke of Atholl, the largest landowner in the area. In total 43 houses were returned to their former glory.

The Little Houses Improvement Scheme was established in 1960 to conserve further properties and, once renovated, these are sold on the open market, but with caveats regarding their maintenance and appearance. The funds accrued are then spend on the acquisition and restoration of other neglected buildings.

DUNKELD HOUSE TREE TRAIL

✉Dunkeld PH8 0HX ✆+44 (0)1738 477400 ⬦pkct.org/dunkeld-birnam

The Trail is situated in the grounds of Dunkeld House Hotel and celebrates the legacy of the 18th-century 'Planting Dukes of Atholl', who owned Dunkeld House Estate and were responsible for creating much of the wooded landscape of this area as we know it today.

The Trail focuses on the heritage of 18 unique trees that grow there, and the Estate is notable in particular for its larches. James Murray, 2nd Duke of Atholl, received some young specimens from the Austrian Tyrol in 1738, and planted them to the west of Dunkeld cathedral. They spawned the many larch trees now to be found all over the vast Atholl estates. The family's interest in woodland and forests continued through the generations, with John Stewart-Murray, 7th Duke, crossing Japanese larches in the late 19th century to produce a hybrid variety.

THE HERMITAGE

✆+44 (0)131 4580200 ⬦nts.org.uk. Located very close to the A9, 1.7 miles north of Dunkeld.

The Hermitage is also the work of 18th-century Dukes of Atholl. Incorporating dramatic natural features such as the Black Linn Falls on the River Braan, this area of forest, complete with very tall Douglas firs, was created purely as a 'pleasure ground', and has been visited by such famous historical figures as the poet William Wordsworth, artist J.M.W. Turner, and composer Felix Mendelssohn.

The Hermitage is now in the care of the National Trust for Scotland, which notes: 'Overlooking the waterfall is the picturesque folly known as Ossian's Hall, built in 1757 as the focal point in an extensive designed landscape. Decorated with mirrors, sliding panels and paintings, it has been refurbished to

▲ *The Hermitage.*

re-create the illusions of shock, surprise and amazement that were the aims of the folly's original design. It makes a fine spot to contemplate the roaring, tumbling falls.'

Niel Gow

Niel Gow is celebrated as one of Scotland's greatest fiddlers and composers of fiddle music. He was born in Strathbraan, south-west of Dunkeld, in 1727, but his family moved to Inver, just over a mile from the town, when he was an infant.

He began playing the fiddle as a child and was soon regarded as one of the best fiddlers in Perthshire, giving up his work as a weaver to play professionally. According to legend, at the age of 18 he entered a musical competition that was being judged by the highly regarded blind musician John McCraw. Niel was awarded first prize, and McCraw declared that he would 'ken his bow hand among a hunder players'.

The Duke of Atholl heard of this and became Niel's patron – giving him an annuity of £5 per year – with the result that not only did the fiddler regularly play for the duke's guests, but was

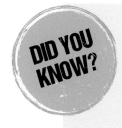

Perthshire is marketed as 'Big Tree Country' by Perth & Kinross Countryside Trust, which states that "With more than 200,000 acres of woodlands, which include more champion trees than anywhere else in the UK, Perthshire is Big Tree Country. Together these create Scotland's most spectacular trees and woodlands, where there are lots of different experiences to discover and enjoy."

The Trust has brought together 18 of the best tree and woodland sights from across the county and grouped them together around seven locations., namely Aberfeldy, Blair Atholl, Crieff & Strathearn, Dunkeld & Birnam, Perth & Scone, Pitlochry, and Rannoch. Visit ⊘pkct.org for details.

also in demand for balls and dances hosted by other members of Perthshire's nobility, playing at venues throughout Scotland.

Niel was married twice, first to Margaret Wiseman, who bore him five sons and three daughters, and, after she predeceased him, to Margaret Urquhart. On her death in 1805, Niel composed what is probably his most famous work, 'Niel Gow's Lament for the Death of his Second Wife'. Niel died at Inver on 1 March 1807, aged 80, and is buried in Dunkeld churchyard.

Members of his family carried on the musical tradition, and Niel's compositions are still widely played today. The annual Niel Gow Scottish Fiddle Festival celebrates his life and work and is staged in Dunkeld during March.

LOCH OF THE LOWES

✉PH8 0PH, tel. +44 (0)1350 727 33 ⊘scottishwildlifetrust.org.uk
Located 2 miles north-east of Dunkeld via the A923 road to Blairgowrie.

Loch of the Lowes is a designated Site of Special Scientific Interest (SSSI), as well as forming part of a Special Area of Conservation. Its Visitor Centre and Wildlife Reserve, which

▲ *Loch of the Lowes.*

covers 370 acres, is best known for the pair of ospreys that nest there from early April until late August. Their eyrie, which has been in use every year since 1991, is situated just 150yds from the Scottish Wildlife Trust's observation hides, and an osprey webcam delivers live footage to the Trust website.

Loch of the Lowes is about much more than ospreys, however, with April to September being the best time to glimpse beavers, while red squirrels, otters, fallow and roe deer, plus varied species of wildfowl, including tufted ducks, goldeneye and great crested grebes, should be visible all year round. Migrant greylag geese roost on the loch during early winter in large numbers.

According to the Scottish Wildlife Trust, highlights include:

- Learning from knowledgeable and enthusiastic staff and volunteers
- Getting closer to the ospreys with binoculars, telescopes and live video footage
- Spotting red squirrels, woodpeckers and other woodland birds from viewing windows
- Joining a ranger-led beaver watch to spot these elusive mammals
- Children's hide – games, books and bird viewing window
- Quizzes, crafts, colouring in, nature draws

- Live and visual interpretation helps bring the story of 50 years of Lowes to life
- Education activities and school visits
- Regular family events throughout the year
- Gift shop stocking a range of wildlife-themed gifts, souvenirs and bird-care products

If you prefer to walk to Loch of the Lowes from near Dunkeld rather than take your car, the Fungarth Walk provides a scenic and moderately energetic alternative, beginning from the Cally car park on the A923. The walk is circular, and stretches for just over five miles (highlandperthshire.org).

ABERFELDY

Heading north from Dunkeld, the A9 shadows the River Tay, until just south of Ballinluig, when the river bears to the west, eventually reaching Loch Tay. Along the way, it passes through the town of Aberfeldy (visitaberfeldy.co.uk), which is definitely worth a detour off the A9 to explore. Take the A827 at Ballinluig, and follow the Tay closely for 10 miles through Strathtay until reaching the attractive market town.

One of the highlights of a visit is the chance to follow the scenic, circular walk known as the Birks of Aberfeldy. 'Birk' is the Scots name for 'birch' and the walk was named after a poem written by Robert Burns in 1787, titled The Birks o'Aberfeldie. The Birks are situated on the western outskirts of the town, and follow the gorge of the Moness Burn, with its multiple waterfalls and ancient birch, ash, oak and elm trees. The extremely scenic walk is 2.25 miles in length and is best accessed from the Birks car park.

Aberfeldy is also home to General Wade's Bridge, which carries the B846 Weem road across the River Tay. The five-arch humpbacked bridge was designed by William Adam and was constructed in 1733, being one of 40 bridges built to the orders of Lieutenant-General George Wade. He was Commander in Chief of His Majesty's Forces in 'North Britain' (Scotland) from 1725, and was responsible for the construction of some 250 miles of roads through the Highlands. The aim was to facilitate rapid movement of soldiers and supplies in the event of another Jacobite rising, following the 1715 attempt to restore a Stuart monarch to the British throne.

Close to the east end of the bridge is the Black Watch Memorial, erected in 1887 to mark the Golden Jubilee of Queen Victoria. The memorial commemorates the first muster of the 42nd Royal Highlanders Regiment – the Black Watch – which occurred on the north bank of the Tay in May 1740. It takes the form of a tall cairn, topped by the figure of Private Farquhar Shaw wearing the original uniform of the regiment.

Just 1 mile west of Aberfeldy, via the B846, is Castle Menzies (✉ Weem, Aberfeldy PH15 2JD ☎ +44 (0)1887 820982 🔗 castlemenzies.org), a 16th-century castle that was the seat of the Chief of Clan Menzies for more than four centuries. During the 1745/46 Jacobite rising Charles Edward Stuart, aka Bonnie Prince Charlie, stayed at the castle while heading to meet his destiny at Culloden Moor (see p.122) in 1746 and, a mere four days later, the castle played host to Charles' nemesis, the Duke of Cumberland.

The ruined castle was restored to its present state by members of the Menzies Clan Society, and since 1993 it has been operated by a charitable trust. As well as serving as a visitor attraction and museum, Castle Menzies is also the clan centre, and special events are staged regularly featuring artists, musicians and craft workers. There is a well-stocked gift shop and snack bar on site.

ABERFELDY DISTILLERY

⌂Aberfeldy, Perthshire PH15 2EB ✎+44 (0)1887 822010 ⌀aberfeldy.com.

Aberfeldy offers a number of tour options:

- The Aberfeldy Distillery Tour (1hr 30min). This includes a guided tour of the production area with its four hissing copper stills, a warehouse visit to experience the maturation process in action, a self-guided exploration of the Heritage Exhibition which gives an insight into the distillery's founders, the Dewar family, and finally a sample of whisky from a choice of three.
- The Cask Whisky Tour (1hr 45min). This includes all elements of the Distillery Tour, plus a sample of whisky straight from a cask in the warehouse, and a complementary branded glass.
- The Whisky Connoisseur Tour (2hrs). Everything that features on the Single Cask Whisky Tour is included, along with an additional whisky tasting mat with five Scotch whiskies from the Aberfeldy and Dewar's ranges.

Aberfeldy is operated by John Dewar & Sons, a subsidiary of owners Bacardi, who also have Aultmore, Royal Brackla, Macduff and Craigellachie distilleries in their portfolio. It was built by the burgeoning Perth-based family business of John Dewar & Sons during 1896/98. By that time, blended Scotch whisky was taking the world by storm, and the new distillery, like so many constructed at the time, was intended solely to provide malt whisky for the company's increasingly popular blends. Today, Dewar's White Label is the best-selling blended Scotch in the USA.

The site chosen for the new distillery was alongside the Aberfeldy to Perth railway line, which provided a direct link into the sidings of John Dewar & Sons' vast bonding and blending facilities in Perth. The company founder, John Dewar, had been born during 1805 in the hamlet of Dull – now twinned with Boring, Oregon! – 3.5 miles west of Aberfeldy. At the age of 23 he joined a relative, Alex MacDonald, in his Perth wine merchant business, setting up in his own right during 1846, with whisky at the core of his retailing activities.

It was his sons, John and Tommy, who were responsible for the creation of Aberfeldy distillery, and the latter was renowned as one of the most flamboyant figures in the Scotch whisky industry. One of the great entrepreneurs of the late Victorian

▲ *Aberfeldy Distillery.*

blended Scotch whisky boom, 'Whisky Tom' sailed yachts and bred racehorses, but he was also a hardworking and charismatic ambassador for the family whisky business, once visiting no fewer than 26 countries in two years to increase its network of agencies. Dewar was also known for his many 'Dewarisms', including 'A teetotaller is one who suffers from thirst instead of enjoying it.'

The distillery boasts a well-equipped shop retailing a wide range of Aberfeldy and other single malts in the same ownership, Dewar's blended whiskies, branded goods and Scottish souvenir items. The principal expressions of Aberfeldy are 12, 16 and 21 years old and the house style is medium-bodied and sweet, with spicy fruit and honey.

BLAIR ATHOL DISTILLERY

✉Perth Rd, Pitlochry PH16 5LY ✆+44 (0)1796 482003 ⊘malts.com

Returning from Aberfeldy to Ballinluig, the A9 north follows the River Tummel for 5 miles until it reaches Pitlochry, bypassed since the 1970s. Take the A924 into the town, arriving first at Blair Athol distillery.

Three tour options are available:

- 'For the Whisky Lover – Master Class Experience': A tutored tasting of four whiskies including Blair Athol's distillery-exclusive bottling and a gift.
- 'For Blair Athol fans – Blair Athol Signature Experience': A guided distillery tour of the production area with its two pairs of stills, followed by a tutored tasting of three whiskies, including the distillery-exclusive bottling and a gift.
- 'For the Connoisseur – Blair Athol Allt Dour Experience': A guided distillery tour followed by a tutored tasting of six whiskies, including one cask strength example drawn straight from the cask, plus the distillery-exclusive bottling and a gift.

One of the few Scottish distilleries that can trace its establishment back to the 18th century, Blair Athol was founded in 1798, and is located not in the village of the same name (spelled with a double 'l' in Atholl) but in south-east Pitlochry, next to the A924 road, formerly the A9.

The distillery was created by John Stewart and Robert Robertson under the 'Aldour' name. The Allt Dour burn runs through the distillery grounds, and translates from the Gaelic as 'Burn of the Otter', which explains the presence of an otter on the label of the 'Flora & Fauna' expression of Blair Athol single malt. The Blair Athol name was adopted in 1825, when Robert Robertson expanded the distillery.

Just as Aberfeldy (see p.79) is the spiritual home of the Bacardi-owned Dewar's blend, so Blair Athol serves as the 'brand home' of Bell's blended Scotch whisky, in the ownership of the world's largest spirits producer, Diageo. Bell's is currently the second-bestselling blended Scotch in the UK after The Famous Grouse.

Bell's had its origins in T.H. Sandeman's Perth wine and spirits business, which a young Arthur Bell joined in 1840, going on to trade in his own right and blend whiskies, utilising Blair Athol malt, along with the 'make' of several other distilleries. By the time Arthur Bell died in 1900, and his son Arthur Kinmont 'AK' Bell took over the firm, the blend was on sale as far afield as India, Australia and New Zealand.

Blair Athol distillery was purchased by Arthur Bell & Sons Ltd in 1933, but due to the prevailing economic climate it remained silent until 1949, when it was substantially rebuilt and re-equipped prior to the recommencement of production. Bell's retained its independence until taken over by the brewer Guinness in 1985, subsequently being absorbed into what was to become Diageo.

Blair Athol single malt is difficult to find, and generally only available in 12-year-old 'Flora & Fauna' format, so a distillery visit gives the rare opportunity to sample a different version in the shape of the distillery-exclusive expression. The house style is aromatic, fruity, honeyed and spicy.

PITLOCHRY

Pitlochrie [sic], a prosperous village in Moulin parish, Perthshire, is situated on the left bank of the river Tummel, and has a station on the Highland railway, 6¾ miles SE of Blair Athole and 12¾ NNW of Dunkeld. Partly from its position, in the midst of and near most romantic and picturesque spots in Highland scenery, and partly from its healthy situation and salubrious climate, the village annually attracts a large number of tourists, visitors, and invalids.
F.H. Groome, Ordnance Gazetteer of Scotland (1882–4)

Most of Pitlochry (⌖pitlochry-scotland.co.uk) as it is today was constructed during the 19th century, and in particular after Queen Victoria's tour of the area in 1842, which did much to popularise it, and the arrival of the railway in 1863. Nearby mountains such as Ben Vrackie and Schiehallion attracted climbers and hillwalkers, as they still do today. A 1920s tourist guide of Pitlochry and its environs describes the town as 'The Switzerland of Scotland', and Pitlochry remains a very popular holiday resort, offering a wide range of accommodation and visitor facilities.

The current main road (A924) through the town was previously the A9, and had its origins in the principal military road north, constructed during the 18th century. The area on the south bank of the River Tummel where the Festival Theatre (see p.84) now stands, known as Port na Craig (Gaelic for 'Port of the Rock'), was the original crossing point of the river from the 12th century onwards. It was established by monks to enable them to access the village of Moulin (see p.87) on the north bank, which dates back to the Bronze Age.

PITLOCHRY DAM VISITOR CENTRE

✉Armoury Rd, Pitlochry PH16 5AP ✆+44 (0)1796 484111
🖱pitlochrydam.com

The Visitor Centre was established in 2017 to showcase the extraordinary story of hydro-electricity in the north of Scotland, with interactive exhibits demonstrating how water can be turned into electric power. However, the dam itself dates back to 1951, when it was constructed as part of the Tummel Hydro-Electric Power Scheme, which comprises nine power stations and reservoirs. The scheme created a new man-made reservoir, Loch Faskally, which is some 2 miles in length and 800yds wide at its narrowest point.

A popular feature of Pitlochry Dam since its earliest days is the 'fish ladder', which enables up to 5,400 examples of Scotland's 'king of fish', the salmon, to ascend to their breeding grounds upriver. The 'ladder' has been used by more than 250,000 salmon since it was built during 1952.

The modern visitor centre includes a gift shop and 60-seat café, and offers views of the active power station and the River Tummel below, while a stunning balcony projects 25ft from the river bank.

PITLOCHRY FESTIVAL THEATRE

✉Port Na Craig, Pitlochry PH16 5DR ✆+44 (0)1796 484626
🖱pitlochryfestivaltheatre.com

Described as 'A unique, theatrical phenomenon in the heart of Perthshire', and 'Scotland's theatre in the hills', the Pitlochry Festival Theatre is located just 350yds downriver from the dam and visitor centre.

The original Festival Theatre was established in 1951 by Glasgow impresario John Stewart, and was based in a series of tents at Knockendarroch, not far from the centre of town. This lasted until the late 1970s, when an entirely new theatre was constructed at Port na Craig, opening for business in May 1981, exactly 30 years after the first performance in the tented structure. The

▲ *Pitlochry Dam and fish ladder.*

current theatre attracts more than 10,000 people per year, and is famous for its Summer Season, when six shows are staged in daily rotation, meaning that visitors can take in a different performance every day, with two on Wednesdays and Saturdays, plus Thursdays through September and October.

The theatre plays host to Christmas musicals and a year-round programme of tours, talks, concerts, events, music and workshops. As the theatre's website states, 'From contemporary comedies to period drama, to musicals and concerts, tours and talks, there is certainly something to suit every taste.'

Adjacent to the Festival Theatre is the Explorers' Garden (✉ Port Na Craig, Pitlochry PH16 5DR ✆ +44 (0)1796 484626 🖰 pitlochry-scotland.co.uk). This celebrates the lives and achievements of Scotland's 'plant hunters', who travelled the world from the 18th century onwards, often experiencing dangerous and challenging conditions in order to collect living specimens or seeds of plants unfamiliar to British gardeners. It is due to their efforts that the likes of roses, lupins, lilies, herbaceous plants, primulas, azaleas, rhododendrons, exotic conifers, shrubs and trees are now familiar sights in our domestic gardens. The Explorers' Garden features a number of 'glades', each devoted to the plants that originated in a different part of the world, and plant hunters commemorated include David Douglas, James Drummond, Archibald Menzies and George Sherriff. The Garden was created in association with the Royal Botanic Garden, Edinburgh.

▲ *The Enchanted Forest.*

THE ENCHANTED FOREST

⌂ Loch Dunmore, Faskally Wood, Pitlochry PH16 5LB
⬀ enchantedforest.org.uk

Through the month of October, off-season travellers on the A9 in Perthshire should try to experience The Enchanted Forest, voted Best Cultural Event at the VisitScotland Regional Awards in 2018 and Best Outdoor Festival at the Scottish Outdoor & Leisure Awards 2017.

The show is created by lighting engineers Simon Hayes and Kate Bonney and sound engineers R.J. McConnell, Rachel Cullen and Jon Beales, who write: 'With dazzling visuals and innovative design set against an original music score, explore the stunning autumn woodland setting of Forest and Land Scotland's Faskally Wood near Pitlochry. Using the forest as a natural backdrop, you

will experience a lighting show that is, quite simply, out of this world.'

Lovers of Scottish beer and whisky should head out of Pitlochry on the A924 towards Bridge of Cally, stopping off initially in the ancient village of Moulin, just a mile north of the town to visit Moulin Brewery (⌂ Moulin PH16 5EW ✆ +44 (0)1796 472196 🖰 moulinhotel.co.uk). The micro-brewery was established during 1995 in a coach-house and stables beside the Moulin Hotel, which celebrated its 300th anniversary that same year. The brewery offers three regular beers, Ale of Atholl, Braveheart and Old Remedial, which are sold on draft in the hotel and a number of other venues in the area, while also being available in bottles. Informal brewery tours are available, along with souvenir items such as branded bottle openers, keyrings, fridge magnets, bar runners and cool bags.

EDRADOUR DISTILLERY

Currently closed to the public. ✉ Balnauld PH16 5JP
☎ +44 (0)1796 472095 🖉 edradour.com

Having sampled beer and brewing at Moulin, continue to follow
the A924 for just over 2 miles, via a signposted local road, to
Edradour distillery, where whisky and whisky-making experiences
await.

If an incurable romantic were to paint a picture of a Highland
distillery, he would surely paint something that looked very like
Edradour. It comprises a cluster of venerable, lime-washed and
red- painted farm-style buildings, grouped around a burn in
the hills. Guided tours of the distillery start with two drams of
Edradour in the Malt Barn, before visitors are shown around this
tiny, hands-on distillery, with the whole experience lasting around
one hour. Tours finish in what the owners claim is the best-
stocked distillery shop in Scotland, where around 25 expressions
of Edradour are on sale, along with much more besides.

Edradour received its first official mention in 1837, operating
as a farmers' co-operative before being formalised as John
MacGlashan & Co in 1841. In 1922 William Whiteley & Co Ltd, a
subsidiary of American distiller J.G. Turney & Sons, purchased
Edradour to provide malt for its blends, which included King's
Ransom and House of Lords. Whiteley subsequently renamed the
distillery Glenforres-Glenlivet.

At this point the history of Edradour becomes as colourful as its
famous red paintwork, with   Whiteley's blends being distributed
in the USA during the Prohibition era by Frank Costello, of
Mafia fame, and on whom the Godfather films were supposedly
based. Indeed, there is strong evidence to suggest that Costello
indirectly owned Edradour for a time from the late 1930s, through
his associate Irving Haim, via J.G. Turney & Sons.

In 1982 Edradour was acquired by the Pernod Ricard subsidiary
Campbell Distilleries, which introduced Edradour as a 10-year-
old single malt bottling four years later. However, in 2002,
Pernod Ricard declared Edradour surplus to requirements, and
independent bottler Andrew Symington of Signatory Vintage
Scotch Whisky Co Ltd paid £5.4 million for the distillery.
Symington has placed great emphasis on releasing Edradour as
a single malt, rather than allowing it to be used for blending, and
in 2003 the distillery also began to produce a peated variant,
marketed under the Ballechin name.

Until the recent proliferation of craft distilleries, Edradour boasted that it was Scotland's smallest distillery, featuring a modest-sized, cast iron open mash tun dating from 1910 and a pair of Oregon pine washbacks, with two stills linked to a 100-year-old condensing 'worm tub'. Then, in 2018, a replica of the original distillery was built on the opposite side of the burn, doubling capacity, and the existing production equipment was subsequently either replaced or refurbished, while additional warehousing was constructed to house the extra whisky being made as it matures.

The principal expressions of Edradour include a 10-year-old, 12-year-old Caledonia, 10-year-old Ballechin, and a variety of bottlings matured in ex-wine casks. Former sherry casks are used for much of Edradour's maturation, influencing the house style, which is sweet and honeyed, with sherry, spice, nuts and malt.

QUEEN'S VIEW AND KILLIECRANKIE

Queen's View is reached by taking the B8019 towards Tummel Bridge off the A9, some 3 miles north of Pitlochry. The road follows the River Tummel to the north shore of Loch Tummel for nearly 4 miles, where the vantage point is located. On a clear day, the views are stunning, stretching along Loch Tummel towards the mountains around Glencoe in the west. Although Queen Victoria visited the location during 1866, it is actually named after Queen Isabella, wife of Robert the Bruce, who reputedly rested there while travelling in the area.

Close by is a Forestry Commission visitor centre, gift shop and café, offering regular screenings of a video featuring local history and wildlife (PH16 5NR +44 (0)1796 474188 forestryandland. gov.scot).

Killiecrankie is the name of a hamlet and a spectacular wooded gorge – or 'pass' – on the River Garry, a tributary of the River Tummel (PH16 5LG +44 (0)1796 473233 nts.org.uk). It is situated 4.3 miles north of Pitlochry via the A924, B8019 and B8079, formerly the A9 before Pitlochry, Killiecrankie and Blair Atholl (see p.92) were bypassed during the 1970s.

Killiecrankie is best known as the location of a bloody battle during the first Jacobite rising of 1689. On 27 July in that year, Jacobite troops led by John Graham of Claverhouse, 1st Viscount Dundee – known in story and song as 'Bonnie Dundee' – defeated a contingent of government troops led by General Hugh Mackay.

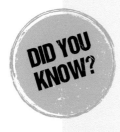

The Atholl Highlanders are Europe's only legal private army, and have the ceremonial role of bodyguard to the Duke of Atholl. They are armed with rifles and boast a well-regarded pipe band.

The Highlanders have their origins in the 77th Regiment of the Foot, raised by John Murray, 4th Duke of Atholl, in 1777 and disbanded just six years later. This followed a regimental mutiny, when the soldiers discovered that far from returning home to Scotland as promised, they were due to be posted to the West Indies.

The regiment was reformed in happier circumstances during 1839 by George Murray, 6th Duke of Atholl under the Atholl Highlanders banner to provide a ceremonial guard for a medieval-style tournament on a grand scale being staged by the Earl of Eglington in Ayrshire.

The Highlanders escorted Queen Victoria on her tour of Perthshire in 1844, during which she stayed at Blair Castle. As a reward for this service, the queen presented 'colours' to the Highlanders, giving them legal status as a regiment.

The Highlanders are composed of around 100 local men with links to the Atholl Estates, and one of the highlights of the year at Blair Castle is the Atholl Highlanders' Ball, staged in the magnificent surroundings of the Victorian ballroom.

▶ *The Atholl Highlanders.*

The Jacobite forces comprised some 3,000 men, while the redcoats numbered around 4,000. The battle took place a mile north of the present National Trust for Scotland visitor centre, and there is a memorial field in the private grounds of Urrard House to commemorate those men who fell during the clash, which was over in around ten minutes.

One of the fleeing government soldiers – Donald MacBean – is reputed to have jumped 18.5ft across the gorge at the point now known as 'The Soldier's Leap', losing a shoe in the process, but surviving and going on to become a prize-fighter. 'The Balfour Stone' is thought to mark the grave of Brigadier Barthold Balfour, a senior officer under General Mackay's command. Despite Killiecrankie being a Jacobite victory, losses were heavy, and 'Bonnie Dundee' was mortally wounded during the battle, being buried at St Bride's Kirk, Blair Castle (see p.94). The Jacobite rising collapsed following defeat at the Battle of Dunkeld (see p.72) the following month.

Today, the Pass of Killiecrankie is in the care of the National Trust for Scotland, and its visitor centre does an excellent job of interpreting the events surrounding the battle, as well as focusing on local geology and wildlife. The Pass is a beautiful and dramatic place to spend time, even if you are not overly interested in Jacobite history. Squirrels, woodpeckers and pine martins are familiar sights, along with the occasional leaping salmon, plus rare mushrooms and toadstools.

BLAIR ATHOLL

The village of Blair Atholl (blairatholl.org.uk) is situated 3.5 miles from Killiecrankie, and is best reached by continuing on the B8079, formerly the A9.

Although dominated by the presence and heritage of Blair Castle (see p.94) the village is well worth exploring in its own right.

ATHOLL COUNTRY LIFE MUSEUM

Old School, Blair Atholl PH18 5SP +44 (0)1796 481232
blairatholl.org.uk

The Museum allows visitors to discover the past of this area and see how previous generations lived. There are three galleries and 28 displays including an old kitchen, complete with box bed, the recreated 1930s Trinafour post office, material relating to school, kirk (church) and smiddy (blacksmith shop), road, rail, gamekeeping and wildlife, plus the doctor's horse sleigh and a collection of horse harnesses. Children can sit in the old school desk, examine the objects in the 'Kiddies Kist', play with the zoetrope or take the quiz and win an award.

WATERMILL AND TEA ROOM

✉Ford Rd, Blair Atholl PH18 5SH ✆+44 (0)1796 481321
🌐blairathollwatermill.com

A mill has existed on this site since at least the 1590s, and it is one of only three working watermills remaining in Scotland. The mill – which is fed by water from the nearby River Tilt – fell silent in 1929 and was used for storage until 1977, when John Ridley began to restore it to working order, passing it on to James and Mary Bruce, parents of the current owner, in 1993.

Today, husband and wife team Kirsty and Rami Cohen grind oats, rye and spelt in the traditional manner. They produce pinhead, coarse, medium and fine oatmeal and coarse wholemeal, rye and spelt flour, plus wholemeal and bread flour. All the grains that are milled are used in the on-site bakery and are available to buy in the tea room.

A variety of home-baked breads, cakes, bagels, rolls and scones are available every day to enjoy in the tea room or take away, and light lunches are also available in the tea room. The Watermill team also offers a series of bread-making courses.

WASTED DEGREES BREWING

✉Unit 11, Sawmill Yard, Blair Atholl PH18 5TL 🌐wasteddegrees.com

If you are looking for something to wash down the mill's fine baking, cross the road to Wasted Degrees Brewing's brewery, tap room and shop. Founded in 2017 by Pitlochry locals, one a teacher and the other an engineer (hence the humorously intended name), Wasted Degrees produces beers inspired by the craft-brewing pioneers from the West Coast of the USA on a 1,000L brew plant. According to the brewers, 'Light malt undertones are backed up by heavy hitting hop character. In addition to our hop-forward range we produce limited releases often utilising local ingredients.'

Bestsellers include canned Hopped Up IPA, Pale Ale and Chipotle Porter, and as well as beer to drink on the premises or take away, the brewery offers a short hot food menu, snacks, wine, spirits and soft drinks, plus branded 'Wasted Degrees' merchandise. Pubic opening times tend to be limited.

BLAIR CASTLE

⌂ Blair Atholl PH18 5TL ✆ +44 (0)1796 481207 ⦿ blair-castle.co.uk

Stunning and majestic in white against a backdrop of woodland and hills, Blair Castle makes a bold statement in the Perthshire landscape. To step inside is to steep yourself in some of the richest and most fascinating history Scotland has to offer. As the Blair Charitable Trust, which owns the castle, puts it, 'Blair Castle gives you the opportunity to see Scottish history through the lives of the Atholl family, their collections of furniture, arms, china, lace and portraits speak for themselves. Over 19 generations the Stewarts and Murrays of Atholl have been adventurers and politicians, Jacobites and Royalists, entrepreneurs and agriculturists, soldiers and scholars. They have made fortunate marriages and have almost all in one way or another made their mark on Blair Castle.'

First impressions are always important, and the Baronial entrance hall, commissioned by John Stewart-Murray, 7th Duke of Atholl in 1872, gives a taste of what is to come. It features a remarkable display of weapons, including muskets and targes (shields) that saw service at the Battle of Culloden. Among the splendid sights to follow are the Tapestry Room, lined with Mortlake Tapestries that belonged to King Charles I and were sold off by order of Oliver Cromwell after the monarch's execution. John Murray, 1st Duke of Atholl, discovered them in Paris and acquired them for the castle.

The tour ends in one of the most impressive spaces in the entire building, namely the Ballroom, commissioned by the 7th Duke, and adorned with antlers, weapons and portraits. This was where the fiddler and composer Niel Gow (see p.74) performed for the Dukes of Atholl and their guests, and his portrait by Sir Henry Raeburn, along with his fiddle and chair, are on display on the ballroom stage.

The earliest known part of the present castle dates from 1269

▶ *Blair castle.*

and is named Comyn's Tower, but in 1740 the 2nd Duke of Atholl began to transform the medieval castle into a Georgian mansion, which covered most of the castle's footprint as it is today. Less radical remodelling took place in the 1860s and '70s when the 7th Duke had turrets and crenellations that had been removed during the Georgian period reinstated. The entrance hall and ballroom were also added at this time.

Remarkably, 19 generations of the Murrays and Stewarts of Atholl have been associated with Blair Castle, and their story and that of their home encompasses Mary Queen of Scots, the Civil War, the Act of Union and Jacobite risings, with Lord George Murray, son of John, 1st Duke of Atholl, taking part in two early uprisings on the side of the Jacobites, before being appointed Lieutenant-General and a senior adviser to Charles Edward Stuart during the 1745–46 conflict.

Queen Victoria also played her part in the story of Blair Castle, staying there for three weeks during 1844, while even the Isle of Man enters the castle's history, as James, 2nd Duke of Atholl, inherited it in 1736, selling it to the British crown for £70,000 in 1765. The present Duke of Atholl – Bruce George Ronald Murray – is the 12th to hold the title, and is resident in his native South Africa.

There is plenty to keep the children happy both inside and outside the castle, including a Castle Detectives Challenge in which children use picture clues to hunt down treasures and work out the answers as they go round the castle, a colouring area in the Treasure Room and a dressing-up box in the Ballroom – providing an opportunity to try on traditional Scottish items of clothing.

Visitors of all ages may explore the grounds, visiting Hercules Garden, a 9-acre walled garden and Diana's Grove, famous for its tall exotic conifers. There are also the ruins of St Bride's Kirk, burial place of 'Bonnie Dundee' (see p.89) to examine, while farm tours, Land Rover safaris and 40 miles of track are available for anyone wishing to explore further. The vast present-day Atholl Estates cover an area from Dunkeld to north of Blair Atholl.

The castle is equipped with a restaurant and gift shop, with the latter stocking clothing, accessories, books, crafts, souvenirs, specialist food and drink, jewellery and children's toys, many of which are based on the Blair Castle collections. It also sells Blair Castle's own china, the 'Evans' collection, and its exclusive blended malt whisky. As well as spending time exploring Blair Castle and its lands, visitors may also stay in a number of houses, cottages, lodges or caravans on the Atholl Estates.

▲ *House of Bruar.*

HOUSE OF BRUAR

✉ By Blair Atholl PH18 5TW ✐ +44 (0)1796 483236 ✐ houseofbruar.com
From Blair Atholl, follow the B8079 road west for 3.5 miles until just
before it re-joins the A9 at Bruar.

The House of Bruar has been nicknamed "The Harrods of the
Highlands". It's impossible to miss it as it occupies a large swathe
of land adjacent to the main road, offering a mix of modern and
traditional architectural styles. It is quite a departure from the
quiet country pub that once stood there.

According to its owners, 'The 11-acre site now plays host
to a Fishing Department, 600-seat Restaurant, Food Hall,
Delicatessen, Butchery, Homewares and Cook Shop, as well as
expansive Menswear and Ladieswear departments which house
the largest collection of cashmere clothing anywhere in the UK.'
There is also an art gallery, which features some of the best in
contemporary Scottish wildlife art and landscape painting.

A large part of the success of House of Bruar is down to the
fact that it has become a destination in its own right, a stand-
alone tourist attraction, rather than just another place to shop. It
has become 'an experience'. This 'experience' – in more modest

form – first opened its doors in 1995 and was the brainchild of entrepreneur Mark Birkbeck, who financed the venture by selling his chain of high street 'Jumpers' stores that he had built up during the 1980s. The Birkbeck family continues to own and run House of Bruar, and in their words: 'The House of Bruar was planned from the outset to showcase the very best in Scottish clothing, produce, art and fashion, bringing together the top brands in the country clothing world to create a shop window for Scotland where tourists and travellers could see the best of what Scotland has to offer in a single upscale retail destination.'

CLAN DONNACHAIDH CENTRE, THE FALLS OF BRUAR

✉Bruar PH18 5TW ✆+44 (0)1796 483770 🌐donnachaidh.com
Situated adjacent to House of Bruar and houses its jewellery collection.

Built in 1969, this was Scotland's first dedicated clan museum, and it contains an absorbing collection of artifacts and records, plus gift items, relating to the clan, which is associated with well-known surnames such as Robertson, Barr, Duncan, Reid, Robb, Roy and Hart.

Access to The Falls of Bruar is situated just behind the main House of Bruar building, and this local beauty spot has become progressively more popular as the renown of House of Bruar has drawn in ever more visitors. After spending time in this area during 1737, Robert Burns penned The Humble Petition of Bruar Water, which is written from the point of view of the waterfall itself, and begs John Murray, 4th Duke of Atholl, to plant trees and bushes along its banks to enhance its natural attractions. The Duke not only did as Burns requested, but also laid the 1.5-mile path still used by walkers to explore the falls today.

North of Bruar the A9 climbs slowly west and north towards the watershed and old county boundary between Perthshire and Inverness-shire, at Drumochter Summit, 1,516ft above sea level. The scenery as the road crosses the Grampians becomes bleakly beautiful, with scree-clad hills and mountains, heather, birch and spruce, all populated by sheep and red deer rather than people.

Drumochter (Gael. druim-uachdar, 'upper ridge'), a mountain pass (1500 feet) over the Central Grampians, on the mutual border of Perth and Inverness shires, 5¾ miles S of Dalwhinnie station, and 2 NNW of Dalnaspidal. Flanked to the W by the Boar of Badenoch (2452 feet), Bruach nan Iomalrean (3175), and Ben Udlaman (3306),

▲ *Steam locomotives 44871 and 45407 reaching Drumochter Summit.*

to the W by Creagan Doire an Donaidh (2367) and Chaoruinn (3004), it is traversed both by the Great North Road from Perth to Inverness and by the Highland railway, being the highest point reached by any railway in the Kingdom. Snow often drifts here to a great extent, lying 30 feet deep in the storm of March 1881.—Ord. Sur., sh. 63,1873.
F.H. Groome, Ordnance Gazetteer of Scotland (1882-4)

The road follows the River Garry for a dozen of the 20 miles between Bruar and the village of Dalwhinnie, and much of this highway dates from the mid-1970s, with construction workers battling through two long, ferocious winters before its opening in 1978.

The eastern extremity of Loch Ericht comes into view to the east of the road, surrounded by distant mountains and with the imposing mass of Ben Alder (3,757ft) towering above it. Dalwhinnie – now on the A889 – stands close to the northern shores of the loch. Near to the Loch Ericht Hotel is a stone bearing the date 1729. It marks the spot where General Wade's road-building troops, working south from Inverness, met up with their counterparts working north from Dunkeld.

The Cairngorms National Park (⌂cairngorms.co.uk) is the largest national park in the UK. It was the second such facility to be developed in Scotland, following the establishment of Loch Lomond and The Trossachs the previous year. Seven years after its creation, The Cairngorms National Park was expanded to take in some of Perth and Kinross.

Kingussie, Newtonmore and Aviemore all lie within the park, which covers some 1,784 square miles, making it larger than the country of Luxemburg! The Cairngorms.co.uk website provides an excellent guide to the National Park and its many attractions, including the project to return beavers to this area.

DALWHINNIE DISTILLERY

⌂Dalwhinnie, Inverness-shire PH19 1AB ✆+44 (0)1540 672219
🖰malts.com

The most prominent feature of Dalwhinnie village, the immaculate white-painted, pagoda-topped Highland distillery is clearly visible from the modern A9, with a backdrop of hills and fir trees. Three tour options are available:

- An introduction to Dalwhinnie with a guided tour: The tour is followed by a tutored tasting of four Dalwhinnie single malts, each paired with a handmade Scottish Highland chocolate (45min).
- Dalwhinnie Whisky & Chocolate Masterclass Experience: 'The ideal tour for chocolate lovers' –tutored tasting of four Dalwhinnie single malts, each paired with a handmade Scottish Highland chocolate (30min).
- Dalwhinnie Expressions Tour & Masterclass Experience: 'The perfect option for whisky connoisseurs' – a guided distillery tour followed by a whisky masterclass of six Dalwhinnie single malts, including the Distillery Exclusive bottling and Special Release, each paired with a handmade Scottish Highland chocolate (1.5hr).

At 1,073ft (327m) above sea level, Dalwhinnie is the second-highest operational distillery in Scotland after Pernod Ricard's Braeval, located south of Glenlivet. One of the duties of the distillery manager is to take readings from the on-site meteorological station.

The distillery dates from 1897/98, just before the great Victorian Scotch whisky 'boom' period turned to 'bust'. It was developed alongside the Perth–Inverness railway line for £10,000 under the auspices of the Strathspey Distillery Co Ltd, originally bearing the name Strathspey. However, just a few months after production commenced in February 1898, the distillery's founders were forced to sell their new plant to A.P. Blyth & Son and John Somerville & Co, who changed the distillery name to Dalwhinnie.

Dalwhinnie had the distinction of becoming the first Scottish distillery to fall into US hands, with Cook & Bernheimer of New York and Baltimore purchasing it at auction for a mere £1,250 in 1905. Dalwhinnie's decline in value reflected the collapse of confidence and activity in the Scotch whisky industry. Cook & Bernheimer operated Dalwhinnie as part of its James Munro & Son Ltd subsidiary, and this name was retained when ownership changed again in 1920, with Sir James Calder buying the distillery.

The Distillers Company Ltd acquired Dalwhinnie six years later, and in 1987 its successor, United Distillers, chose Dalwhinnie 15-year-old as part of its Classic Malts range. A visitor centre opened four years later. The distillery – now owned by Diageo – is equipped with a single pair of stills and is unusual in that spirit is condensed not by 'shell and tube' condensers, as is now commonplace, but by a pair of large wooden 'worm tubs' that are a notable feature of the distillery exterior.

Dalwhinnie is one of Diageo's best-selling single malts and a key component of the popular Buchanan and Black & White blended Scotch brands. The Dalwhinnie line-up consists of a 15-year-old, a Distillers Edition variant (finished in oloroso sherry casks) and Dalwhinnie Winter Gold. The house style is sweet and honeyed, medium-bodied, fruity and spicy.

NEWTONMORE AND KINGUSSIE

Newtonmore (⊘newtonmore.com) is the first of the two villages to be reached when heading north on the A9 (via the A86 exit), some 14 miles beyond Dalwhinnie, and, like nearby Kingussie, it has been bypassed since 1979. Between Newtonmore and Kingussie the former A9 is now the A86.

Newtonmore is home to two excellent museums, see below.

CLAN MACPHERSON MUSEUM

⊡Main St, Newtonmore PH20 1DE ✐+44 (0)1540 673332
⊘clanmacphersonmuseum.org.uk. The museum is located at the south end of the village.

This museum opened in 1952 and '...boasts a large collection of artefacts and other objects of historical importance. The collections are significant to the Highlands of Scotland and to members of the Macpherson Clan in particular. The layout of items in the Museum is organised in chronological order, enabling a story to be told through objects, documents and text as you make your way round. There is an audio-visual presentation provided at the start of the Museum's circuit and this gives visitors insight into the clan system and the Macpherson Clan.'

One particularly notable member of the clan was Ewan 'Cluny' MacPherson (1706–64), chief during the Jacobite rising of 1745/46 and an avid supporter of Charles Edward Stuart and the Jacobite cause. MacPherson raised some 600 men to fight for the Stuarts, and in reprisal his home was burnt and his possessions looted by government troops following the Jacobite defeat at the Battle of Culloden (see p.122). Cluny was forced to take to the hills, and legend has it that he hid for nine years in a cave – known as 'Cluny's Cage' – high on Ben Alder, though the 'Cage' may have been a man-made structure and its exact location remains unclear.

Prince Charles Edward Stuart is known to have stayed with MacPherson for several days before eventually escaping to France and MacPherson also managed to reach France, where he was reunited with his family before his death in Dunkirk.

▶ *Highland Folk Museum.*

HIGHLAND FOLK MUSEUM

Aultlarie Croft, Kingussie Rd, Newtonmore PH20 1AY ✆+44 (0)1349 781650 ⌂highlifehighland.com. Situated on the northern outskirts of Newtonmore.

The museum was created by folklorist and historian Dr Isabel Frances Grant (1887–1983) and was originally located on the island of Iona, where it opened in 1935 with the name 'Am Fasgadh', Gaelic for 'The Shelter'. Before too long, the museum had outgrown its home there, moving to a disused church at Laggan, Inverness-shire during 1939. Grant began to search for a more permanent location for the collection and was able to purchase three acres of land in Kingussie, where the museum opened its doors in June 1944.

Three replica buildings, including a Hebridean 'blackhouse', were constructed on the site, and machinery, tools and household objects were displayed in lifelike settings to give visitors a real feeling of life in the Highlands during times past. Isabel Grant's collection had the distinction of being mainland Britain's first open-air museum.

Highland Council subsequently acquired the museum and

▲ *Ruthven Barracks.*

during the early 1980s proceeded to re-establish it on its present 80-acre site, which is split into four principal areas: Aultlarie Croft, a 1930s working farm, Balameanach (Middle Village) with a developing community of relocated buildings, the Pinewoods, and 'Baile Gean', the Museum's reconstruction of an early 1700s Highland township.

Most of the buildings within the Museum were in danger of being demolished, and they include a smoke house, school, church, clockmaker's workshop, croft house, post office, railway halt and joiner's shop. As the Museum's administrators explain, 'On this mile-long site visitors can discover how Highland people lived, worked and dressed, how they produced food, cooked and what they ate from the 1700s up to 1950s.'

The Museum is equipped with a café, gift shop and the novel feature of Kirk's Store Sweetie Shop – a traditional sweet shop named after the Kirk family who farmed Aultlarie Croft.

Continue on the A86 for 3 miles and you arrive in Kingussie. Newtonmore and Kingussie may be close neighbours, but there is a fierce sporting rivalry between the two villages, and this centres around the uniquely Highland sport of shinty. Not unlike Ireland's hurling, shinty is played by two teams of 12, and each player is armed with a caman, or curved stick, which is used to strike the

small leather ball. The game can become very physical and is administered by the Camanachd Association, with the highlight of the shinty season being the Camanachd Cup, first competed for in 1895. Teams from Newtonmore and Kingussie have historically been among the top sides in the world of shinty, each collecting a great deal of silverware in the process.

The area around Newtonmore and Kingussie is known as Badenoch and Strathspey, and the famous River Spey flows close to the A9 here, with the road crossing the river near Kingussie. As well as the Spey, another sight visible from the A9 is the dark brooding ruin of Ruthven Barracks, see below.

RUTHVEN BARRACKS

✉ PH21 1NR ⊘ historicenvironment.scot
Accessed by the B970 from Kingussie centre.

Ruthven Barracks were one of four such structures built by King George II's government between 1719 and 1721 as part of a military response to the Jacobite rising of 1715. The elevated site chosen commanded a wide view of the surrounding area and had been the location for a castle built in 1229, which was later home to the notorious 'Wolf of Badenoch', Alexander Stewart, Earl of Buchan and a son of King Robert II. A new castle was created on the site between 1451 and 1459, and this was seriously damaged by John Graham – 'Bonnie Dundee' – during the Jacobite rising of 1689.

The barracks that were subsequently created comprised two substantial three-storey blocks occupying two sides of the enclosure, and bastion towers were constructed at opposite corners. The government troops stationed there came under an unsuccessful attack from Jacobite forces in August 1745, but the following year, a numerically superior contingent of Jacobite soldiers laid siege to the barracks, leading to surrender of the garrison.

Follow the B970 from Ruthven Barracks for just over a mile to reach

SPEYSIDE DISTILLERY

Tromie Mills, Glentromie, Kingussie PH21 1NS +44 (0)1479 810126 speysidedistillery.co.uk), which is open to the public on limited occasions. At other times, the associated 'Snug' in Aviemore (see p.113) retails the full range of distillery bottlings and will arrange tastings.

The site of the distillery was originally a barley mill and croft dating back to the 1700s, and although the date when the first spirit flowed from Speyside's pair of stills was December 1990, the 'founding' year could easily be stated as 1956 or 1962. This is because 1956 was when Glasgow whisky broker George Christie bought the site on the banks of the River Tromie, three miles from the town of Kingussie, and 1962 was the year in which dry-stone waller Alex Fairlie actually began construction of the distillery. Building proceeded on a somewhat leisurely basis, taking just short of three decades and, once completed, Christie's project was christened Speyside, which may seem slightly generic but was actually the revival of an old, local distillery name. The original Speyside distillery had been established in Kingussie during 1895, though it only operated for a decade before falling into disuse.

The 'new' Speyside may have taken a long time to build, but it did not take long for the spirit it produced to find its way into bottles, with the first release of The Drumguish single malt taking place in 1993, when the whisky could only have been just legally Scotch whisky.

A decade after the Speyside stills were fired up ownership passed to a group of private investors, including the founder's son, Ricky Christie, and in 2012 the long-established firm of Harvey's of Edinburgh assumed control, going on to create an entirely new range of whiskies. These include Spey Trutina (matured in Bourbon casks), Spey Fumare (made from peated barley), Spey Temme (finished in tawny port casks), Spey Chairman's Choice (matured in a mix of sherry and Bourbon casks), and Spey Royal Choice (comprising whisky from some of the distillery's oldest casks).

The house style is medium-bodied and floral, with malt, dried fruit and nuts, and in addition to its single malts line-up, the Speyside distillery also now distils gin, marketed under the Byron's Gin banner.

From the Speyside distillery, either continue on the B970 and re-join the A9 close to Aviemore, or retrace your steps to Kingussie and follow the B9152 for 4.3 miles to the Highland Wildlife Park.

HIGHLAND WILDLIFE PARK

✉Kincraig, Kingussie PH21 1NL ✆+44 (0)1540 651270
🖥highlandwildlifepark.org.uk

The park plays host to more than 200 examples of Scottish wildlife and endangered animals of the world's mountains and tundra regions. Visitors drive through the Main Reserve and then explore the 'walk-round' area on foot. As its owners explain, 'The Wildlife Park has a wide and diverse range of animals, from native species such as the capercaillie and Scottish wildcat to those from further afield such as the Amur tiger and polar bear.'

Among the animals housed in the Main Reserve are elk, bison, wolves, yaks and Bactrian camel, while in the walk-round enclosures are Scottish wildcat, northern lynx, red panda, Arctic fox, Japanese macaque, Chinese grey goral, European beaver, wolverine, musk ox, capercaillie, snowy owl, great grey owl and Eurasian eagle owl.

The park attracted lots of headlines in late 2017, when the first polar bear to be born in the UK for 25 years arrived just before Christmas. After a popular vote, he was given the name Hamish, and in October 2020 he moved to the Yorkshire Wildlife Park's Project Polar habitat. However, December 2021 saw the birth of another cub, named Brodie, who is proving an equally popular attraction. Besides polar bears, the park also welcomed its first litter of snow leopards in 2019.

SCOTTISH WILDLIFE

As the team at Scotland.org put it,

"Magnificent mountains, atmospheric glens, dramatic coastlines, picturesque lochs and rivers and fabulous forestry: no wonder Scotland's scenery has a reputation for being among the most spectacular in the world."

This scenery is also home to a fascinating and diverse range of wildlife. Indeed, there are more than 90,000 species living in the country.

Here is a selection of iconic ones to look out for – some more elusive than others!

VISIT www.scottishwildlifetrust.org.uk for more information.

RED DEER

The Red Deer (*Cervus elaphus*) – and particularly the Red Deer stag - is almost as synonymous with Scotland as shortbread or tartan, captured at its most noble in Edwin Landseer's magnificent painting 'The Monarch of the Glen.' The stags boast large, branching antlers, which increase in size with age. The Red Deer is the UK's largest land mammal and is to be found on moorlands, mountains, and grasslands in most parts of rural Scotland, including the Cairngorms National Park. The best time to see them in the wild is during the autumn months, when the breeding season, or 'rut' takes place..

RED GROUSE

A sub-species of the Willow Grouse, the Red Grouse (*lagopus lagopus scoticus*) is unique to the British Isles, and is found all year round on Scottish heather moorland. It is one of four grouse species, along with the Black Grouse – which frequents lower scrub and rough grazing land - Ptarmigan and Capercaillie. Commercial shooting of Red Grouse during the season that starts on the

'Glorious Twelfth' of August provides major economic benefits for the Scottish economy. The Red Grouse is notable for lying low until approached then 'exploding' out of the heather at great speed.

PTARMIGAN

The Ptarmigan (*lagopus mutus*) is the smallest of the four grouse species. It is a hardy bird, which lives all year round on hilltops in the Highlands. It is the only British bird that changes colour to protect it from predators such as eagles, becoming predominantly white in winter in order to be camouflaged by snow. There are concerns that numbers may fall in the long term due to climate change which is leading to less snow fall in the Scottish Highlands

CAPERCAILLIE

The largest of the game bird family. The species is protected by law due to declining numbers. They live in pine forests and are renowned for 'lekking' in spring, which involves males parading and making a remarkable range of hissing, wheezing, cork-popping sounds to attract females. Fights between males are common.

RED SQUIRREL

Scotland has become a haven for the red squirrel, as its larger non-native grey counterpart has displaced it across much of Britain. 75 per cent of the UK's Red Squirrel population is now to be found in Scotland, but even here, numbers have declined significantly. The Grey Squirrel carries the squirrel pox virus which does not harm them, but is deadly to its red cousin. Red Squirrels are found across much of the country and are most easily spotted during winter months, when their distinctive coats stand out from the snow.

WILDCAT

'The Highland Tiger' as it is sometimes nicknamed has almost been wiped out by predation, habitat loss and interbreeding with domestic felines. The species is now so critically endangered that sixteen wildcats have been paired up at the Highland Wildlife

Park (see p.75) near Kingussie as part of the Saving Wildcats initiative. Kittens will be released into the wild in the Cairngorms during 2023 onwards. The Scottish Wildcat (*Felis silvestris silvestris*) tends to live in mixed woodlands and is heavier than its domestic relation, with longer limbs with striped fur and tabby patterning.

SALMON

The Atlantic salmon (*Salmo salar*) is closely associated with the rivers of Scotland, and its pursuit makes an important contribution to the rural economy of the country. Atlantic salmon live in freshwater as juveniles but migrate to sea as adults before returning up river to spawn. Remarkably, they return to their native river, and even the same stretch of the water where they were born, with astonishing accuracy. According to Scottish Government statistics, the total reported rod catch of wild salmon for 2020 was the third lowest on record. As numbers have declined overall in recent years, 'catch and release' policies have been widely implemented.

OSPREY

The Osprey (*Pandion haliaetus*) was hunted to near extinction in Scotland by the early years of the 20th century, but in 1954, a programme of recolonisation began at Loch Garten RSPB Reserve (Nethy Bridge PH25 3EF) in the Cairngorms. It remains one of the best places in Scotland to see this large bird of prey, along with the Loch of the Lowes Visitor Centre and Wildlife Reserve (see p.75). Ospreys nest hundreds of feet above the ground in isolated locations, so only the really fortunate are lucky enough to glimpse of one diving dramatically into a river or loch to catch a fish. There are now thought to be between 250 and 300 breeding pairs of Ospreys across Scotland.

GOLDEN EAGLE

The Golden Eagle (Aquila chrysaetos) is described by the Scottish Wildlife Trust as "The top predator in the Scottish countryside; it is a massive bird of prey that mainly hunts rabbits and mountain hares but will also catch foxes, young deer and large birds like grouse." The Golden Eagle has an average wingspan of almost seven feet (2.1 metres) and inhabits remote glens and moorland areas, building nests on rocky cliff faces or in trees, where their large nests are known as eyries. Golden Eagles are rare birds and a sighting of one is a clear highlight of time spent in the Highlands

The A9 has been associated with what remains the UK's longest-running missing persons' case, following the disappearance of Inverness resident Renee MacRae and her three-year-old son Andrew in November 1976.

Mrs MacRae's BMW car was discovered on fire in a layby on the A9 close to Dalmagarry Quarry, south of Inverness, but despite a number of large-scale searches over the intervening years, no bodies have ever been discovered.

However, in September 2019, Renee MacRae's 79-year-old former lover William McDowell, of Penrith, Cumbria, was charged at Inverness Sherrif Court with her murder and that of her son. He stood trial in September 2022 and was found guilty, being sentenced to life in prison, with a recommendation that he serve a minimum of 30 years. He died in prison, the following year.

After viewing the amazingly diverse range of animals and birds in the park, visitors may relax over a hot or cold light meal in Antlers Coffee Shop, situated within the visitor centre and offering great views over the Japanese snow monkey enclosure to the Spey valley beyond. As an alternative, The Oystercatcher is located close to the visitor centre and offers teas, coffees, soft drinks and snacks. Finally, no visit would be complete without souvenirs to take home, and the Wildthings shop offers 'an extensive range of local and wildlife related-gifts to suit all ages and all pockets including some exclusive line and polar bear-themed gifts'.

The Highland Wildlife Park opened in 1972, and since 1986 has been owned by the Royal Zoological Society of Scotland (RZSS), which also operates Edinburgh Zoo. In 1980, the park made headlines after taking in a puma, named Felicity, that was allegedly captured by a local farmer, and since 2007 there has been something of a change of emphasis from showcasing purely native Scottish breeds to those – often endangered – species from mountain and tundra regions all over the world.

AVIEMORE AND CARRBRIDGE

From Kincraig, continue on the B9152 which runs parallel to the east of the A9 for just under 10 miles to Aviemore (⌖visitaviemore.com). Before entering Aviemore village, it is worth making a short detour via the B9710 to Rothiemurchus, see below.

ROTHIEMURCHUS

✉Rothiemurchus Centre, by Aviemore, PH22 1QH ✆+44 (0)1479 812345 rothiemurchus.net

The Rothiemurchus Estate comprises almost 25,000 acres of ancient Caledonian forest, lochs, rivers, glens and mountains, and has been owned by the Grant family since the 16th century. It offers a wide range of outdoor activities, including mountain biking, Segway adventures, pony trekking, clay shooting, fishing, river tubing, rafting and paddle-boarding, a ranger-led Hairy Coo Safari and a Highland Lady Tour by Land Rover.

The 'Highland Lady' in question was Elizabeth Grant of Rothiemurchus (1797–1885), whose book *Memoirs of a Highland Lady* – written between 1845 and 1854 – provides a fascinating insight into the life of a young woman of aristocratic birth, and in particular of a great Highland estate, during the early 19th century.

For more ambitious outdoor activities, continue from Rothiemurchus via Coylumbridge to Glenmore Lodge, see below.

GLENMORE LODGE

✉Aviemore PH22 1QZ ✆(0)1479 861 256 glenmorelodge.org.uk

In its role as Scotland's national outdoor training centre, Glenmore offers 'world class training in outdoor adventure sports' and aims to 'encourage more people to enjoy the outdoors more often'. Residential courses include Summer Rock & Mountain, Summer Alpine, Winter Mountain, Mountain Biking, Backcountry Skiing and Paddlesports. There is also a fully equipped gym, climbing wall, climbing towers and dry tool climbing wall, a dry ski slope, and the intriguingly titled Avalanche Transceiver Park.

▲ *Mountain biking on the Rothiemurchus estate.*

GLENMORE FOREST PARK
PH22 1QU forestryandland.gov.scot

Close to Glenmore Lodge is Glenmore Forest Park, which boasts a visitor centre with café and a range of trails and activities such as orienteering. Picturesque Loch Morlich – over 1,000ft above sea level – with its popular beaches is a short walk away.

Within the park is the Cairngorm Reindeer Herd (cairngormreindeer.co.uk), Britain's only free-ranging herd of reindeer, which numbers around 150 animals in total. There is a dedicated shop and a daily guided Hill Trip to see the reindeer up close. You can even adopt one for yourself!

CAIRNGORM MOUNTAIN SKI AREA

+44 (0)1479 861261 cairngormmountain.co.uk
South-east of Glenmore Lodge and the Forest Park.

This is most popular skiing centre in the UK, along with the best access routes to scale all 4,000-plus feet of Cairngorm itself. According to Cairngorm Mountain (Scotland) Ltd: 'Home to skiers as early as the late 1890s in Coire Cas, Cairn Gorm has long been synonymous with winter snow-sports. During the 1950s the Cairngorm Sports Development Fund was set up to try and establish commercial skiing, and ever since has welcomed hundreds of thousands of visitors to its slopes.'

The Cairngorm funicular railway opened in 2001, but closed in 2018 due to structural problems. However, Highlands and Islands Enterprise (HIE), which owns the railway and wider Cairngorm Mountain snow sports centre, carried out repairs to the UK's highest railway at an estimated cost of £10 million, and it reopened early in 2023, though there have been subsequent closures.

Originally little more than an inn on the old military road, Aviemore was a relatively quiet Highland village until the early 1960s, although the arrival of the railway in the mid-19th century had allowed it to become a quiet holiday resort. The development of commercial skiing close by in the Cairngorms during the 1950s and '60s and the installation of a ski lift led to rapid development of Aviemore into an Alpine-style resort at the cost of £3 million, with the Aviemore Centre opening in 1966. The village became the UK's first dedicated ski resort and is now a bustling place all year round.

▲ *Locomotive 46512 running on The Strathspey Railway.*

THE STRATHSPEY RAILWAY

⌂ Aviemore Station, Dalfaber Rd, Aviemore PH22 1PY
✎ +44 (0)1479 810 725 ✐ strathspeyrailway.co.uk

Operating on a 10-mile restored section of the old Highland
Line between Aviemore and Broomhill via Boat of Garten, the
Strathspey Railway was created in 1978 with the mission to return
steam train travel to the Highlands.

Today, trains run from platform 3 of Aviemore station and
ticketing is flexible to allow travellers to break their journeys at
Boat of Garten or Broomhill and explore the beautiful surrounding
countryside. Broomhill was built to serve the nearby villages of
Dulnain Bridge and Nethy Bridge on the original Great North of
Scotland Railway line, and had a role in the popular TV series
Monarch of the Glen as Glenbogle Station.

THE SNUG

✉ Retail Park, Santa Claus Dr, Aviemore PH22 1AF ✆ +44 (0)1479 810126
🖥 thesnugspeysidedistillery.co.uk

The Snug is affiliated with Speyside Distillery, and according
to the distillers, it is 'built in a style to reflect that of Speyside
distillery itself – old wooden beams, stone walls and a hand-
crafted bar made from our whisky barrel staves – and you are
welcomed into a cosy environment.'

The Snug is home to the full range of Spey single malts and
other spirits, along with art and craft items. Tasting events in
the Snug, or even on the Strathspey Railway (see p.116), may be
booked, along with distillery visits.

CAIRNGORM BREWERY

✉ Dalfaber Dr, Aviemore PH22 1ST ✆ +44 (0)1479 812222
🖥 cairngormbrewery.com

The brewery was established in 2001 and now boasts a 20-barrel
brewhouse with the capacity to produce 6,500 litres of beer
per day. Ten bottled beers are permanently available, from the

Alistair Stuart MacLean (1922 - 1987) was a best-selling author, noted for books such as The Guns of Navarone and Where Eagles Dare. Although born in Glasgow, he was brought up in Daviot, 12 miles south of Inverness and in sight of the modern A9. His father, also Alistair, was the local minister. The novelist was buried in Switzerland, but a memorial to him was erected in Daviot Parish kirkyard.

continental-style Cairngorm Gold via the strong and complex Wildcat to a mahogany ale named Stag, and Cairngorm beers are also on draught in a wide range of bars and hotels across the Highlands. The permanent range is backed up by seasonal brews, and tasting sessions and brewery tours are offered on a regular basis. There is also a well-stocked brewery shop, selling Cairngorm and Loch Ness beers, along with branded merchandise.

AVIEMORE KART RACEWAY

⌂Granish, Aviemore PH22 1QD ✆+44 (0)1479 812079
✐aviemorekartraceway.co.uk
Located some 4.5 miles north of Aviemore, via the A9.

The raceway offers outdoor go karting experiences for all the family, with three types of family karts: 120cc, 200cc and tandems, for one adult and one child, while anyone over 17 can take part in adult-only sessions on more powerful 270cc karts. 'Arrive and Drive' karting is available in 10-minute time trials, and multiple 10-minute time trials per driver may be purchased for family karting or adult sessions.

▲ *Landmark Forest Adventure park map.*

LANDMARK FOREST ADVENTURE PARK, CARRBRIDGE

Follow the A9 for 6 miles from Aviemore and you come to the by-passed village of Carrbridge (⌖carrbridge.com).

Carrbridge is famous for its distinctive packhorse bridge, built across the River Dulnain in 1717, and the oldest stone bridge in the Highlands. It is also home to the World Porridge Making Championship, staged there annually since 1996. The event attracts entrants from all over the world, keen to lift the coveted Golden Spurtle trophy. Each September 'Carve Carrbridge' sees contestants armed with chainsaws show how artistic they can be with a large log of wood.

Landmark Forest Adventure Park (✉Carrbridge PH23 3AJ ✆+44 (0)1479 841613 ⌖landmarkpark.co.uk) is located just south of the village, on the B9153, which connects Carrbridge with the A9. The park comprises 30 acres of native pinewood which are home to 17 individual attractions for all the family. As the owners note: 'Climb aboard our Runaway Timber Train family rollercoaster for a twisty ride among the pines and after that you can try "waterfall rafting" on the thrilling "Wild Watercoaster". Kids love "Ant City" adventure play centre, mini cars, remote controlled trucks and mini diggers. The "Wild Forest Maze" is a fun challenge for all. Discover "The Timber Trail" with the UK's only steam-powered Sawmill. And how about stepping up to the top of the giant Forest Viewing Tower with amazing views to the mountains all around.'

▲ *Bottle-your-own in the Tomatin distillery visitor centre.*

Other attractions include The Red Squirrel Nature and Treetop Trail, the Tarzan Trail treetop ropes course and the Skydive 'parachute jump', not to mention Dinosaur Kingdom and the Tropical Hot-house, plus a wildlife feeding area which regularly attracts red squirrels.

After all the activity, The Foresters Restaurant and the Pinewood Snack Bar offer home-cooked meals and snacks, and the Landmark Shop is filled with souvenirs and toys which reflect the park's outdoor adventures, wildlife and forestry themes. The park really deserves half a day or more of anyone's time, and weekly and seasonal family tickets are available.

Back on the A9, the road rises towards Slochd Summit (1,382ft), which marks the boundary between the Spey Valley and the Inverness area of the Highlands Region. It is the second-highest mountain pass on the A9 after Drumochter, and can be a challenging drive during winter snowstorms. North of the pass is the by-passed hamlet of Tomatin, home to a distillery that is very popular with visitors.

TOMATIN DISTILLERY

Tomatin, Inverness-shire IV13 7YT +44 (0)1463 248144
tomatin.com

There are a number of tour options, with the most popular being
the Legacy Tour, which allows visitors to explore the distillery
and discover its history, with a post-tour tasting of three Tomatin
single malts (1hr 15min). There is also a bottle-your-own option in
the visitor centre, where you may fill an exclusive cask-strength
expression of Tomatin. The centre's gift shop stocks the definitive
range of Tomatin whiskies and branded merchandise.

Tomatin distillery is located among the bleakly beautiful
moorland scenery of the Monadhliath Mountains, 15 miles north of
Aviemore and 16 miles south of Inverness. Winters can be harsh
here, and there is a real sense of this being a distilling community
rather than just a workplace. There are some 30 houses on
site, mostly occupied by staff members, and the distillery even
boasts its own on-site engineer to emphasise the sense of self-
sufficiency.

Tomatin was established in 1897, during the great Victorian
whisky 'boom' of the late 19th century, and was principally used as
a component of blended Scotches until recent times. The rather
industrial appearance of Tomatin can be explained by post-World
War II expansion programmes, beginning in 1956 when a second
pair of stills was installed. By 1974 no fewer than 23 stills were in
place, theoretically able to produce some 12 million litres of spirit
per year, making it by far the largest malt distillery in Scotland in
terms of capacity. Not that Tomatin ever reached full capacity,
as the distillery achieved its peak potential just as the Scotch
whisky industry was beginning to wake up to the fact that over-
production was creating a crisis, with what journalists were quick
to dub the 'whisky loch' filling up at an alarming rate.

When distillers began to tighten their belts in the early 1980s,
Tomatin Distillers plc closed down the 'number two side' of the
still house, before entering receivership in 1985. The following
year, Tomatin became the first Scottish distillery to be wholly
owned by Japanese interests, and in 2002 11 stills were removed,
leaving six pairs currently in use, giving an annual capacity of 5
million litres.

The core Tomatin range comprises Legacy (no age statement
and matured in a combination of Bourbon barrels and virgin oak
casks), a cask strength version (no age statement and matured in

a combination of Bourbon barrels and sherry casks), plus 12-, 14-, 18-, 30- and 36-year-olds. The Warehouse 6 collection comprises a number of rare, aged vintages and there is even a 50-year-old bottling if you are feeling really extravagant.

For some years, peated batches of spirit have been produced, and since 2013 peated Tomatin has been branded Cù Bòcan (cu-bocan.com). Tomatin itself is marketed as 'the softer side of the Highlands', and the house style is medium-bodied, malty, with spice, honey and very delicate smoke.

CULLODEN BATTLEFIELD

Culloden Moor, Culloden, Inverness IV2 5EU ✆ +44 (0)1463 796090
nts.org.uk The battlefield is located 5.5 miles east of the city of Inverness, via the B9006 from the A9.

Culloden Battlefield was the scene of the last pitched battle to be fought on British soil, and the moor is home to the graves of the 1,500 Jacobites and 500 government soldiers who died in the encounter on 16 April 1746. Visitors may walk along the battle lines and see the soldiers' graves alongside the memorial cairn. Clan markers indicate the graves, and flags represent the front lines of both armies, giving a clear sense of the large scale of the battle.

Despite achieving victory at the Battle of Falkirk on 17 January 1746, the Jacobite army led by Charles Edward Stuart was forced to retreat further north by government forces, finally establishing a base at Inverness. Ignoring advice to undertake a guerrilla campaign, Charles opted to engage with the government army, led by the Duke of Cumberland, son of King George II, in a pitched battle on Drumossie Moor, Culloden. The Jacobite troops numbered around 6,000, while Cumberland commanded some 8,000 men.

Charles had been warned that the boggy ground of the moor would favour Cumberland's men if the Jacobites were to charge the enemy lines, and this proved to be the case. The battle was over in less than one hour, leaving 300 government casualties, but between 1,500 and 2,000 Jacobite dead and injured. In the aftermath of the battle, Cumberland earned the nickname 'Butcher Cumberland' in the Highlands, due to the brutality with which he hunted down and killed Jacobite survivors and their supporters. The remnants of the Jacobite army who escaped Culloden rallied at Ruthven Barracks (see p.105), but the last Jacobite rising ended on Culloden Moor.

Culloden Visitor Centre houses a 360-degree 'battle immersion theatre', which uses technology to bring the battle to life in a remarkably vivid way. The action can be followed up on a 'battle table', which helps explain the tactics used by both armies. Rare artefacts from the battle are also on display, including the magnificent Brodie Sword and a blunderbuss removed from the battlefield by a government soldier. There are also archaeological finds, including musket balls, buckles and a poignant Jacobite cross made from pewter.

The early 18th-century Leanach Cottage stands near the modern visitor centre, and having been inhabited until 1912, it was later restored as the battlefield's first visitor centre. The cottage is constructed from stone and turf, with a roof thatched with heather sourced from the battlefield itself. The visitor centre café specialises in using local produce, and offers full meals, snacks, traybakes, and cheese and charcuterie platters. The well-stocked shop retails exclusive Culloden Ale and Culloden Battlefield Highland Single Malt whisky, along with local chutneys, jams, shortbread, books, clan-related products and jewellery, including Scottish silver jewellery from Botanic Isles containing flowers picked on the battlefield itself.

INVERNESS AND LOCH NESS

highlifehighland.com.
Boethius [Roman senator, c.AD 447–524] relates, that in his time Inverness was greatly frequented by merchants from Germany, who purchased here the furs of several sorts of wild beasts; and that wild horses were found in great abundance in that neighborhood [sic]: that the country yielded a great deal of wheat and other corn, and quantities of nuts and apples. At present there is a trade in the skins of Deer, Roes, and other beasts, which the Highlanders bring down to the fairs. [end quote]
Thomas Pennant, A Tour in Scotland, 1769 (London: Benjamin White, 1776)

Inverness – or Inbhir Nis in Gaelic – is located almost exactly halfway between Perth and Scrabster, and is often referred to as 'the capital of the Highlands'. The settlement is an ancient one, with St Columba visiting King Brude at his fortress there during the 6th century AD, while in 1040 Macbeth reputedly murdered King Duncan on the site of the present Inverness Castle.

Inverness became a royal burgh early in the 12th century, during the reign of King David I (ruled 1124–53), who also built

▲ *Inverness castle.*

a new castle there. King William I (ruled 1165–1214) went on to grant the town four charters later in the same century, and medieval Inverness was a prosperous place due principally to fishing and trading activities, involving the export of wool, fur and hides. In the 1650s, Oliver Cromwell built a citadel there during his occupation of Scotland, and Inverness continued to be an important garrison and hub for the network of military roads that spanned the Highlands from the early 18th century onwards.

Inverness gained city status in 2000, and it stands at the northern end of the Great Glen – a fault line complete with a series of lochs that were joined together to form the Caledonian Canal – which links Fort William on the west coast to Inverness in the east. The River Ness provides a picturesque feature as it flows through the city.

The creation of the Caledonian Canal by Scottish engineer Thomas Telford during the early years of the 19th century increased trade in Inverness due to its enhanced accessibility, and when the railway arrived in 1855, that accessibility increased significantly, leading to many tourists visiting Inverness and the surrounding Highlands.

INVERNESS MUSEUM AND ART GALLERY

⌂ Castle Wynd, Inverness IV2 3EB ✆ +44 (0)1349 781730,
🖰 highlifehighland.com

The museum showcases aspects of Highland history and
culture. The building dates from the 1960s and houses
geological, archaeological and natural history exhibits, as well
as a fascinating array of Jacobite memorabilia, weapons and
bagpipes. The work of local artists and crafters is also on display.

INVERNESS CASTLE

⌂ IV2 3EG ✆ +44 (0)1349 781730 🖰 highlifehighland.com

The castle is situated not far from the Museum and Art Gallery, on
a cliff overlooking the River Ness. The pink sandstone structure
actually comprises two crenellated buildings, with the first being
constructed as a courthouse during the 1830s, while the second
was built in the following decade as a jail.

   The present castle occupies the site of a medieval structure
which was re-fortified to house government soldiers during the
early 18th century, and was destroyed by Jacobite troops prior
to the Battle of Culloden (see p.122). The original well that served

the medieval fortress survives in the grounds of the castle, and a striking sculpture of Flora MacDonald, who helped Charles Edward Stuart escape to France, looks out over the Ness. It was created during the 1890s by local sculptor Andrew Davidson.

Until 2020, Inverness Castle continued to serve as a court house, but with the construction of a new Justice Centre, plans were formulated to reimagine the castle as a major tourist attraction, with work ongoing at the time of writing.

UILE-BHEIST DISTILLERY

⌂Ness Bank, Inverness IV2 4SG ✆+44 (0)1463 234308
🖉www.uilebeist.com

Uile-bheist is a combined brewery and distillery located close to Inverness Castle and the city centre, on the banks of the River Ness. Uile-bheist - pronounced EWL-uh vehst, from the Gaelic for 'monster' - referencing the Loch Ness Monster – offers a range of visitor experiences relating to both whisky and beer.

The 'entry level option is the Discovery Tour, which involves exploring both brewery and distillery, with whisky and beer offerings included, while the Boilermaker and Tasting version adds a tasting of core Uile-bheist beers and global whisky chasers. An alternative adds a selection of cheeses into the mx, while the Blending Experience offers participants the chance to blend and bottle their own whisky at the end of the tour.

The ultimate Uile-bheist experience is the Master Maker's Tour, conducted by master brewer and distiller Bruce Smith, culminating in a sampling session of Uile-bheist beers and whisky chasers. A range of whisky and beer flights, representing both the Scottish malt whisky regions and the wider whisky world, is also available. Overall, a selection of up to 250 whiskies from all over the world is being assembled at Uile-bheist to make it a whisky-lover's destination in its own right.

Until the 1980s, Inverness was home to three whisky distilleries, namely Glen Mhor (established in 1846) and Glen Albyn (founded in 1892), both located beside the Caledonian Canal, plus Millburn (dating from 1807). Unfortunately, all fell victim to the over-capacity of the Scotch whisky industry at that time. Happily, however, whisky-making returned to the city in the spring of 2023 courtesy of husband-and-wife hoteliers and restauranteurs Jon and Victoria Erasmus.

The site uses an innovative water source heat pump to harness

▲ *Uile-Bheist distillery.*

heat from water drawn from the River Ness along with solar panels to generate electricity. This provides heating and hot water services for not just Uile-bheist but also the associated Glen Mhor hotel, apartments and the Erasmus' nearby Waterside restaurant.

The whole ethos of Uile-bheist is based around reimagining myths and legends from local folklore, and striking artwork on these themes has been created by Melbourne-based illustrator and designer Ken Taylor, famed for his pop culture images and striking rock posters produced for the likes of Metallica, Bob Dylan and The Rolling Stones.

All brewing and distilling equipment was supplied by German brewery experts Kaspar Schultz, who fabricated their first pair of Scotch whisky stills for Uile-bheist. Mashing takes place in the brew kit for two days each week, leaving the brewer with the other five days in which to make beer.

The spirit being produced is light in character, with between 200 and 250 casks filled during the first year of operation. While the Uile-bheist team waits for the single malt to mature, some 'new-make' will be bottled for sale, along with a 'spirit blend' named Colpach.

ABERTARFF HOUSE

71 Church St, Inverness IV1 1ES +44 (0)131 385 7490, nts.org.uk

The house was built in 1593 and is the oldest surviving house in Inverness and an important example of 16th-century domestic architecture. It features distinctive crow-stepped gables and a projecting turnpike stairway. The building was once the townhouse of the Frasers of Lovat, who fought on the Jacobite site during the 1745/46 rising, and in the 19th century it was owned by the Commercial Bank of Scotland. Later divided into a number of housing units, Abertarff subsequently became semi-derelict, before being given to the National Trust for Scotland in 1963. Restoration took place three years later to return the house to its original splendour. An exhibition reveals some intriguing aspects of the 'hidden history of Inverness in the 1600s'.

INVERNESS BOTANIC GARDENS

Bught Ln, Inverness IV3 5SS +44 (0)1463 713553
 highlifehighland.com

The gardens are the UK's most northerly botanic gardens and offer horticultural attractions whatever the season. Formal gardens, ponds, a tropical house, a cactus house and a wild flower meadow are all part of what has been described as 'a green emerald in the heart of the city'.

To the rear of the site, and entered through a ramshackle gate, is the Secret Garden with its G.R.O.W project (Garden, Recycle, Organic and Wildlife). During the past two decades adults with special needs have turned what was once waste ground into a productive garden, and sales of plants help to keep the charity-run Botanic Gardens in business.

▲ *Eden Court Theatre.*

EDEN COURT

✉ Bishop's Rd, Inverness IV3 5SA ✆ +44 (0)1463 234234
🌐 highlifehighland.com

This is Scotland's largest combined arts organisation and is housed in three connected buildings that stand by the banks of the River Ness. Eden Court was established in 1976 and expanded between 2004 and 2008, now boasting an 869-seat theatre named The Empire and the 275-seat On Touch Theatre. There are also two cinemas, three art galleries and two multi-purpose studios.

As well as producing and presenting work inside the arts complex, the Eden Court team erect a large stretch tent, complete with stage and bar, in the grounds of Eden Court each summer, and also take productions and exhibitions on the road around the Highlands.

The Gaelic language and culture are showcased in a Gaelic and Traditional Arts programme, and Eden Court also boasts a shop, bar and well-regarded restaurant.

CLANS & TARTANS

"What is tartan? Essentially, it is woollen cloth woven in one of several patterns of coloured checks and intersecting lines, especially of a design associated with a particular Scottish clan."

VISIT www.tartansauthority.com

Ask anyone in virtually any country in the world what they most associate with Scotland and they will say 'tartan.' Indeed, tartan has become something of a cliché, shorthand for a tourist's view of Scotland, but it is an important part of the nation's heritage and also its present. As such, it deserves to be celebrated and cherished.

FIRSTLY, JUST WHAT IS TARTAN?

Essentially, it is woollen cloth woven in one of several patterns of coloured checks and intersecting lines, especially of a design associated with a particular Scottish clan.

SECONDLY, JUST WHAT IS A CLAN?

The word is derived from the Gaelic 'clann,' meaning children, and the clan system of society had its roots in Celtic, Norse or Norman-French traditions. By the 13th century, the system was firmly established in the Highlands and islands of Scotland, and some of the historically most influential clans include Campbell, MacDonald, MacGregor, Macleod, and Robertson.

According to the Society of Antiquities of Scotland, "A Scottish clan...is a kinship group among the Scottish people. Court of the Lord Lyon regulates Scottish heraldry and coats of arms. It is a common misconception that every person who bears a clan's name is a lineal descendant of the chiefs.

"Many clanspeople although not related to the chief took the chief's surname as their own to either show solidarity, or to obtain basic protection or for much needed sustenance. Most of the followers of the clan were tenants, who supplied labour to the clan leaders.

"Many clans have their own clan chief. Scottish clans generally identify with geographical areas in Scotland originally controlled by their founders, sometimes with an ancestral castle and clan gatherings, which form a regular part of the social scene today."

Clan chiefs were extremely influential figures, with a great deal of power within the territory they controlled, and the clan system survived across the Highlands and islands of Scotland until the aftermath of the Battle of Culloden in 1746 [see page 122].

In an attempt to frustrate future rebellions, the British government introduced an Act of Proscription, which outlaws the playing of bagpipes, the wearing of clan tartans and the speaking Gaelic.

That from and after the first day of August, One thousand, seven hundred and forty-seven, no man or boy within that part of Britain called Scotland, other than such as shall be employed as Officers and Soldiers in His Majesty's Forces, shall, on any pretext whatever, wear or put on the clothes commonly called Highland clothes (that is to say) the Plaid, Philabeg, or little Kilt, Trowse, Shoulder-belts, or any part whatever of what peculiarly belongs to the Highland Garb; and that no tartan or party-coloured plaid of stuff shall be used for Great Coats or upper coats, and if any such person shall presume after the said first day of August, to wear or put on the aforesaid garment or any part of them, every such person so offending
Abolition and Proscription of the Highland Dress 19 George II, Chap. 39, Sec. 17, 1746.

William Grant Foundation research fellow Rosie Waine of the National Museum of Scotland explains that "Highland dress underwent a dramatic transformation during this period, because while it was banned in Scotland because of its Jacobite associations it was never banned in the British Army. It was used very much as a military uniform by serving Scottish soldiers.

"It was an elite group of Scots who

▲ *Pipe band at The Ballater Highland Games.*

were living in London who formed the first Highland Society and got the Dress Act repealed. There was then a national movement to recover Highland dress from its years in exile and make it an emblem, not just of Scotland, but of Scotland within the British Union."

From the point of view of clan structure, however, improved communications and more widespread trade and movement of people during the second half of the 18th century and early 19th century were already eroding its influence. The 'Highland Clearances,' in which tenants were displaced from their homes, with many emigrating as a result, really marked the end of the clan system.

Not surprisingly, many of the descendants of those who left the Highlands and islands for new lives in North America, Australia and New Zealand are keen to trace their Scottish heritage and The Scottish Tartan Authority (tartansauthority.com) is the ideal place to start exploring.

Every clan has its own official tartan, or tartans, and central to the use of tartan is the kilt. After decades of being associated with establishment figures of a certain age, Highland dress, and specifically the kilt, has been reclaimed by younger Scots who wear it with pride, and not just when attending weddings or sporting occasions.

Some of the credit for making the kilt 'cool' is due to films such as the 1995 duo

Rob Roy and Braveheart, and more recently the multiple television series of Outlander, but Highland dress had previously enjoyed a period of wide popularity during the 19th century. This was largely attributable to the widespread appeal of Sir Walter Scott's epic poems such as The Lady of the Lake (1810) and historical novels like Waverley (1814).

Tartan mania had its highpoint during the visit of King George IV to Scotland in 1822, when Scott was tasked with orchestrating the occasion. Highland dress was very much central to events celebrating the first visit to Scotland by a British monarch in nearly two centuries. The king ordered a Highland outfit in bright red tartan, subsequently known as Royal Stuart tartan, and the outfit itself, and

accessories, cost the grand sum of £1,354 18s, now equivalent to around £130,000.

Today, tartan is celebrated all over the world, and New York even hosts an annual Tartan Week devoted to Scottish events and activities, culminating in a vast tartan-clad, bagpipe-paying parade. The essential appeal of tartan is easy to appreciate, capturing the popular imagination because of its romantic, colourful appearance, variety and genuine historical provenance in Scottish life and culture.

INVERNESS VICTORIAN MARKET

⌂Academy St, Inverness IV1 1JN ✆+44 (0)1463 710524,
⊘thevictorianmarket.com

Dating from 1870, the market follows the Victorian trend for
replacing existing open-air markets with new covered facilities.
In June 1889, the market was destroyed by a major fire, but a
programme of reconstruction meant that it was able to reopen in
September 1891.

Today, the market is a bustling and characterful place, boasting
cafés and an eclectic mix of small shops, including butchers,
jewellers, gift shops, fashion accessory outlets, Highland dress
outfitters, and even a bagpipe supplier.

THE NORTHERN MEETING

⊘northern-meeting.org

The Northern Meeting dates back to June 1788 when 13 Highland
gentlemen set out to liven up the social life of the area by
sending out invitations to 110 people inviting them to take part
in an annual meeting 'for the purpose of promoting a Social
Intercourse'. By October, 74 gentlemen and three ladies had
applied to become members, with their number principally
comprising the local gentry and well-to-do Inverness professional
businessmen and merchants.

Today, the Northern Meeting hosts a grand ball each summer,
and less formal 'reel parties', lunches and cocktail parties
throughout the year. More significantly for the public at large,
however, it organises a solo piping competition which is staged
in early September, and is recognised as the most prestigious
competition for solo pipers from around the world.

INVERNESS HIGHLAND GAMES

⊘invernesshighlandgames.com.

The Northern Meeting was also responsible for the Inverness
Highland Games, staged over a weekend in July, but these now
have a separate identity. They are held in the world's oldest
Highland Games stadium, Northern Meeting Park, and commence
with the Highlands Strongest Man and Strongest Woman
Championships. The 'heavy' events are always a highly popular
feature of any Highland Games, and comprise the shot put,

tug-o-war, caber toss and hammer throw. Unique to Inverness is a remarkable lifting event, dating back to 1822. This involves the Stonemason's Stone, which weighs 252lb and has to be lifted cleanly over a bar suspended 5ft in the air. Fewer than a dozen athletes have been able to perform the feat!

As well as all the high-energy events taking place, the Games also host Scotland's largest inter-clan gathering, Highland dancing, a craft fair, fun fair, traders' village, Armed Forces displays and solo piping competitions organised by the Inverness Piping Society. A parade around the city and the fabled RuffNess Dog Show round off events on the Sunday.

If you are not able to get to Inverness for this spectacular weekend, Highland Games are staged throughout the Highlands during the summer months and are organised by the Scottish Highland Games Association. Its website (shga.co.uk) gives full details of upcoming events and much more besides.

SECTION THREE
Inverness to Scrabster

Inverness	138
Glen Ord distillery	139
Beauly and Dingwall	140
Black Isle Brewery	142
The Clootie Well	142
Alness and Invergordon	143
Dalmore distillery	145
Tain	147
Glenmorangie distillery	149
BREAKOUT: SCOTCH WHISKY	150
Balblair distillery	154
Dornoch	155
Historylinks Museum	156
Dornoch Cathedral	156
Dornoch distillery	157
Royal Dornoch Golf Club	158
Dornoch Beach	158
The Mound and Golspie	159
Dunrobin Castle	161
Clynelish and Brora distilleries	163
Helmsdale	164
Ord of Caithness, Badbea and Berriedale	166
Dunbeath	167
Dunbeath Heritage Centre	168
The Laidhay Croft Museum	168
Thurso	169
Wolfburn distillery	170
North Point Distillery	171
Scrabster	172
Clan Gunn Heritage Centre & Museum	174
Lybster	174
The Waterlines Heritage Centre	174
Grey Cairns of Camster	175
Whaligoe Steps	175
Wick	176
The Castle of Old Wick, Sinclair and Girnigoe	178
Pulteney distillery	179
The Caithness Broch Centre	182
8 Doors Distillery	183
The Castle of Mey	187
Dunnet Bay distillery	188
The Seadrift Centre	189

INVERNESS – LATHERON - 87 MILES
LATHERON TO SCRABSTER - 57 MILES

TOTAL DISTANCE - 114 MILES

North of Inverness, while some towns such
as Beauly, Dingwall and Bonar Bridge have
been bypassed, much of the A9 remains
as it did during the 1970s, with single
carriageway and only the very occasional
re-aligned sections or overtaking lanes.
Heading through Sutherland and into
Caithness, quite closely following the coast,
hills and mountains are left behind. Indeed,
Caithness is sometimes described as 'The
Lowlands beyond the Highlands.'

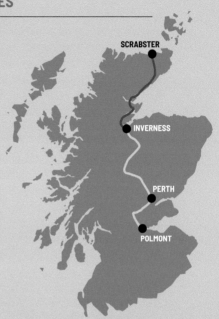

SCRABSTER

INVERNESS

PERTH

POLMONT

WHERE TO STAY

Hotels
Tain
The Glenmorangie House
⌂ glenmorangie.com
Carnegie Lodge Hotel
⌂ carnegiehotel.co.uk
Helmsdale
Belgrave Arms Hotel
⌂ belgravearmshotel.co.uk
Wick
Mackays Hotel
⌂ www.mackayshotel.co.uk
Thurso
Pentland Hotel
⌂ pentlandhotel.co.uk

Caravan/Glamping/Campsites
Tain area
Dornoch Firth Caravan Park
⌂ dornochfirth.co.uk
Wick area
Wick Campsite
⌂ wickcampsite.co.uk
Caitness Camping Pods
⌂ caithnesscampingpods.com
Thurso area
Thurso Bay Caravan and Camping Park
⌂ thursobaycamping.co.uk

INVERNESS

This is the starting point for the North Coast 500 (⌖northcoast500. com) which "brings together a route of more than 500 miles of stunning coastal scenery – 516 miles, to be exact. Not only is the NC500 one of the world's best road trips, but it's also one of the most beautiful. While the North Coast 500 is an experience in itself, you'll also find plenty of adventures to be had along the way."

The route was inaugurated in 2015 and starts at Inverness Castle (see p.125), following the A9 to Thurso, before heading west to Durness near Cape Wrath in the far north-west of Sutherland, and returning to Inverness via Ullapool and Dingwall.

Travelling south from Inverness via the A82, the northern shores of Loch Ness (⌖invernesslochness.com/ ⌖lochness.com) are located some six miles away. The loch is 24 miles long, one mile wide on average, and deeper than the North Sea. It is, of course, known the world over as home to the Loch Ness Monster, or 'Nessie,' if you wish to be less formal. According to legend, St Columba was the first person to see the elusive long-necked, hump-backed creature, way back in the 6th century, and ever since that first sighting, monster hunters have been drawn to the loch to try to catch a glimpse for themselves.

One great way to experience Loch Ness – and possibly make a sighting of Nessie - is by taking to the water. **Jacobite Cruises** – ☏+44 (0)1463 233999 - ⌖jacobite.co.uk - operate four vessels from several locations close to Inverness city, allowing you to experience the loch in all its glory, with snacks, soft drinks and a licensed bar on board each boat.

Until the opening of the Kessock Bridge, which spans the narrow strip of land that separates the Inverness and Beauly Firths in 1982, the A9 passed through the heart of Inverness, which provided a major bottleneck on the same sort of scale as Perth during busy holiday periods.

However, a ferry had operated across the Beauly Firth between Inverness and South Kessock from the 15th century, and only ceased running in July 1982, when the bridge opened to traffic.

The 'old' A9 crossed the Caledonian Canal and Lovat Bridge as it exited Inverness, running east of the city to the town of Beauly (see p.140) before heading north via Muir of Ord to Dingwall (see p.140), close to the Cromarty Firth. The replacement road cut some 14 miles off the route between Inverness and the A9 along the north-west shore of the Cromarty Firth to Alness (see p.144).

Creating the Kessock Bridge and a dramatically realigned A9 that

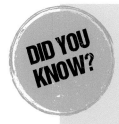

During construction of the Kessock Bridge, a steel erector made a bet with his foreman that he would be the first person to drive across the bridge. As this seemed extremely unlikely to happen, the foreman accepted the wager. The following day, the workman arrived with a golf ball and a golf driver and drove the ball across the 30 feet gap between the two spans of the incomplete bridge to win his bet.

ran across the fertile area known as the 'Black Isle' – actually a promontory between the Moray Firth and the Cromarty Firth - to a new low-level bridge over the Cromarty Firth meant that Beauly and Dingwall were left somewhat isolated, compared to their previous busy location astride the A9.

Both are well worth a detour – via the A832 and A862 roads from the Tore Roundabout, and Glen Ord distillery is also accessed by the A832.

GLEN ORD DISTILLERY

Glen Ord Distillery, Muir of Ord, Ross-shire IV6 7UJ +44 (0) 1463 872004 malts.com

The distillery is situated seven miles west of the Tore roundabout on the A9 north of Inverness, accessed via the A832. The Diageo-owned distillery contributes significantly to the Johnnie Walker family of blended Scotches, while its single malt is extremely popular in Asian markets.

Following major upgrading work during 2022, Glen Ord's visitor centre now serves as a brand home for the three Singleton single malts – Ord, Dufftown and Glendullan – and features a new bar area and accompanying delicatessen. Three tour options are available, including whisky and food pairing, and the Malt to Cask Experience, which allows rare opportunity to visit the maltings adjacent to the distillery.

Little known in the UK and mainland Europe, Glen Ord has become something of a cult single malt in the Far East and especially Taiwan, thanks to re-formulation and rebranding as 'Singleton of Glen Ord in 2006, having previously been sold as Glen Ord, Ord and Ordie. Interestingly, it was recorded during the 1880s that South Africa and Singapore were significant export markets for the whisky.

Glen Ord distillery is located in fertile farmland to the west of Inverness and dates back to 1838, when it was established by Thomas Mackenzie. Through a number of owners, Glen Ord came into the possession of John Dewar & Sons Ltd in 1923, and when Dewar's joined the Distillers Company Ltd (DCL) two years later, the distillery was one of the assets transferred to DCL's Scottish Malt Distillers subsidiary.

Along with many other DCL malt distilleries, Glen Ord was virtually rebuilt during the 1960s, when the complement of stills was increased from two to six, all housed in one of the distinctive glass-fronted stillhouses which make a DCL plant from the period instantly recognisable today.

Glen Ord's capacity has grown in recent years, and it now boasts no fewer than 14 stills and the ability to make up to 11.9m litres of spirit per annum, making it Diageo's second-largest malt distillery after Roseisle, near Elgin.

From a blending perspective, the distillery produces spirit that is green, grassy, fruity, waxy and oily in character, and the stills are run slowly but very hot in order to capture pure, intense 'grassy' spirit.

As well as Glen Ord distillery, the site has been home to a maltings plant since 1968, and in addition to providing malt for Glen Ord itself, a number of other Diageo distilleries are served by this facility, including nearby Teaninich, Clynelish and Talisker.

The Singleton of Glen Ord range comprises 12, 15 and 18-year-old variants, and the house style is fruity and spicy, grassy and oily, with toffee and vanilla.

BEAULY AND DINGWALL

The quickest way to reach Beauly IV4 7BY (⌀visitbeauly.com) is via the A9 to the Tore roundabout, some 15.6 miles north of Inverness, and then the A832 and A682 for 7.3 miles to reach the village.

The origins of Beauly date back to the establishment of the – now ruined - priory in 1230 by John Byset of the Aird, for Valliscaulian monks. One suggested origin of the name Beauly is from the reaction of Mary Queen of Scots, who stayed there overnight in 1564. She is said to have exclaimed "C'est un beau lieu" – what a beautiful place. However, the name is more likely to derive from the French monks from Burgundy who inhabited the priory, as they had another foundation south of the border in Hampshire named 'Beaulieu.'

The village as it appears today, with its attractive broad square was laid out in 1840, and is located beside one of Scotland's most renowned salmon fishing streams, the River Beauly. The surrounding area was once the domain of the Lovat Frasers, who lived at Beaufort Castle and owned large amounts of land. The castle and much of the land was sold in 1994 by Simon Fraser, 15th Lord Lovat, to settle debts. The Lovat Frasers feature prominently in the novels and television series of Outlander, bringing a whole new wave of interest to the story of the clan and its colourful history.

From Beauly, follow the A682 and A835 for 10 miles to Dingwall (Inbhir Pheofharain in Gaelic), a Royal Burgh which occupies a strategically significant location at the head of the Cromarty Firth and was first developed as a settlement in Norse times.

Although little evidence remains today, Dingwall was once an important port, with a harbour constructed by the renowned Thomas Telford c. 1820. One hint at its maritime past is provided by the presence of a starfish on the town's coat of arms.

Until major reorganisation during the 1970s, Dingwall was the county town and administrative centre of Ross & Cromarty, which embraced a large swathe of land, including the Outer Hebridean Isle of Lewis!

The town was based around a castle, constructed during the 13th century, when it was the largest fortress north of Stirling (see p.33). The structure was reputedly on the site of the castle in which Macbeth was born c.1010, though the last remnants of the fortifications have long since disappeared beneath civic buildings.

The rivers Beauly and Conan were spanned by bridges in 1814 to the south of Dingwall, leading to the town's role as a communication hub, with new roads being constructed to the north and west. The construction of the railway line north from Inverness by the Inverness and Ross-shire Railway (I&RR) brought train services to Dingwall in July 1862. The station went on to become an important junction for the line north to Wick and Thurso (now named the Far North Line) and the line west to Kyle of Lochalsh, a role it still plays today.

BLACK ISLE BREWERY

✉Allangrange, Munochy IV8 8NZ ✆+44 (0) 1463 811 871
🖫blackislebrewery.com

Black Isle Brewery is well signposted off the A9 between
Inverness and Tore roundabout. It is Scotland's only organic
brewery, founded back in 1998 by David Gladwin, when the
British craft beer boom was in its infancy. Black Isle can brew
up to 10,000 litres a day, packaged in bottles, casks and kegs,
and available not only throughout Scotland, but as far afield as
Norway and Japan.

Organic barley for beer-making is grown on the 125-acre farm
attached to the brewery, along with seasonal vegetables, herbs
and salads, which are used in the brewery's Black Isle Bar, located
on Church Street in Inverness, and boasting a superb beer menu.
The farm is also home to 200 black Hebridean sheep and a Jersey
'house cow.' The farm has a long heritage of producing high-
quality crops, with Sir Roderick Mackenzie recording in 1790 that
the land was first cultivated for growing barley because it was of
"superior quality for the brewer and distiller."

There are regular brewery tours, and the brewery shop stocks
an extensive range of Black Isle branded merchandise, and core
and specialist bottled and canned beers. Popular beers in the
regular range include Blonde, Goldfinch, Red Kite and Porter.

THE CLOOTIE WELL

Back on the A9 after a detour to Black Isle Brewery, head north
to the Tore roundabout and take the A832 towards Munlochy for
2.25 miles to reach the Clootie Well car park, marked by brightly
coloured rags or cloths ('cloots') around the entrance (✉IV8 8PE).

The Clootie Well harks back to pre-Christian days, when
pilgrims would visit reputedly holy wells, which were said to have
healing properties. The well at Munlochy may date from around
AD620, when St Boniface was performing missionary work in
Scotland. Pilgrims would circle the well before saying a prayer and
splashing well water on the ground, then tying
an item of clothing or rag that had been touched by the person
who was afflicted to a nearby tree. Tradition has it that the illness
would be cured as the 'cloot' rotted with time.

Although the practice of visiting holy wells survived the arrival

▲ *Black Isle Brewery farm with some of their Hebridean sheep.*

of widespread Christianity in Britain, it tended to be frowned on by religious bodies due to its pagan origins and was actually made illegal by a Scottish Act of Parliament in 1581. However, as can be seen by a visit to the Clootie Well at Munlochy today, pilgrims of one sort of another clearly still make their way to this woodland site on the Black Isle.

ALNESS AND INVERGORDON

North of Tore roundabout, the A9 crosses the Cromarty Firth by way of the Cromarty Firth Bridge and is joined at a roundabout by the A862 from Dingwall. From here, the A9 follows the course of the pre-1970s road construction projects for some miles, shadowing the north-west shore of the Cromarty Firth, which is often home to oil rigs either undergoing maintenance or 'resting' between global assignments. The health of the world's oil exploration industry at any one time may be gauged by the number of rigs lying idle at significant expense in this ideally sheltered, deep-water anchorage. At night, the illuminated rigs make a splendid sight, like a surreal village in the middle of the Firth.

The town of Alness (⌀alness.com) is serviced by the B176 off the A9, and is located on both sides of the River Alness, also known as the Averon. It was serving as a significant port on the Cromarty Firth by the late 17th century. The creation of a road in 1715, complete with ferry crossing of the river, led to the growth of the settlement, and in 1810 the first bridge over the river was constructed, while Thomas Telford significantly improved the quality of the road.

Today, a Heritage Centre (102 High St, Alness IV17 0SG ✆+44 (0) 1349 883005) does a great job of interpreting the social history of the area, and the town boasts two working distilleries, namely Teaninich, founded in 1817, operated by Diageo and not open to the public, and Dalmore (see p.145).

A notable landmark close to Alness is the Fyrish Monument, built on Fyrish Hill during 1782 at the behest of local Sir Hector Munro, who funded it as a 'job creation scheme' for locals. The monument is a replica of the Gate of Negapatam, an Indian port, which Munro had captured for the British in 1781, when serving as a general.Just three miles from Alness via the B817 is Invergordon (⌀visitinvergordon.com), which for centuries was the northern crossing point for a ferry across the Cromarty Firth, taking pilgrims to St Duthac's chapel at Tain (see p.147). The Gordon family took the settlement to the next level, laying out a planned town during the 18th century, while a dedicated harbour was built during 1828.

Given its status as a superb natural harbour, Invergordon became a naval base just before the outbreak of the World War I in 1914, and Dalmore distillery (see p.145) was repurposed as a mine assembly facility in 1917, named US Navy Base 17, with the star- spangled banner flying over the distillery during the last months of the war.

In World War II, the Cromarty Firth was once again of strategic importance, and land to the west of Dalmore was taken over by the RAF in 1942 to allow an expansion of their Invergordon base, with the firth being home to Sunderland and Catalina 'flying boats.'

Invergordon was also the scene of a notorious naval mutiny in 1931 when stringent pay cuts were proposed. Invergordon Naval Museum & Heritage Centre (140 High St, Invergordon IV18 0AE ⌀invergordonmuseum.co.uk) is a great place to explore local maritime history in depth. Today, visiting cruise ships provide an important source of revenue to the port and surrounding area.

Firth of Cromartie'[sic]: "Ride along a very good road cut on the side of a hill, with the country very well cultivated above and below, with several small woods interspersed near the water's edge. There is a fine view of almost the whole bay, the most capacious and secure of any in Great Britain ; its whole navy might lay there with ease, and ships of two hundred tuns may sail up above two-thirds of its length, which extends near thirty English miles from the Sutters of Cromartie 171 to a small distance beyond Dingwall : the entrance is narrow; the projecting hills defend this fine bay from all winds..."
Thomas Pennant, A Tour in Scotland 1769 (London: Benjamin White, 1776)

DALMORE DISTILLERY

⌂Alness, Ross-shire IV17 0UT ✆+44 (0) 1349 882362 ⌕thedalmore.com
The distillery is located less than a mile from Alness via the B817 but due to the creation of a new production area, there is no public access to Dalmore until 2025

Prior to its temporary closure to the public, the visitor facilities included a 'museum' room which explores the heritage of the distillery and characters associated with it. Highlight of the distillery tour is the marvellously quirky stillhouse and two drams of single malt are offered at its conclusion in the luxurious tasting room. Branded items and a wide range of The Dalmore whiskies are available in the distillery shop.

Dalmore distillery was established on the shores of the

▲ *A vintage truck at the Dalmore distillery.*

Cromarty Firth in 1839 by Alexander Matheson, who had made a fortune in the opium trade. Matheson gave over the running of his distillery to various estate tenants, and in 1867 Andrew Mackenzie and his family took the reins. The Mackenzies eventually bought Dalmore from the Matheson family in 1891 for £14,500, by which time the number of stills had been doubled to four.

The distillery remained in the Mackenzie family until 1960, when Mackenzie Brothers (Dalmore) Ltd merged with the Glasgow blending firm of Whyte & Mackay Ltd, who were longstanding customers for Dalmore single malt. In 1966, with the Scotch whisky industry booming, another four stills were installed to double capacity.

The stillhouse is one of the quirkiest in Scotland, featuring four flat-topped wash stills of diverse shapes and sizes and four spirit stills with 'boil-balls' and distinctive cooling copper water jackets, while a section of 'number two spirit still' dates back to 1874.

Dalmore's transformation during the past two decades from well-regarded single malt to one of the two most collectable and highly-prized whiskies in Scotland has been a remarkable one. Along with The Macallan, The Dalmore is able to release extremely limited editions of very old whisky and sell them for the sort of sums many rival distillers can only dream of. In May 2020, two bottles of 62-year-old The Dalmore sold at auction for a record-breaking price of £266,200 each!

The Dalmore is characterised by its full-bodied, richly sherried house style and its ability to flourish during extended periods of ageing, as evidenced by bottlings up to 64 years of age. The principal casks used for maturation are first-fill ex-Bourbon barrels and former sherry butts, with Dalmore being the only Scotch whisky distillery with access to Matusalem Oloroso sherry butts from the historic house of Gonzales Byass.

Core bottlings include 12, 15, 18 and 25-year-old expressions, along with Port Wood Reserve and Cigar Malt Reserve. There is also Dalmore 1263 King Alexander III, which takes its name from the fact that in 1263 an ancestor of the Clan Mackenzie saved King Alexander III from being gored by a stag. The stag's head duly became the Clan Mackenzie motto, and adorns all expressions of The Dalmore.

TAIN

Fourteen miles north of Alness on the A9 is the now-bypassed (via the B9174) royal burgh of Tain (⌗tain.org.uk), which was granted a royal charter in 1066 by King Malcom III, making it the oldest royal burgh in Scotland. The charter also proclaimed it a place of sanctuary where the protection of the church could be invoked and resident traders were not required to pay certain taxes.

The origins of the settlement are likely to be Viking, and central to its history is St Duthac, born there around 1,000. Accounts differ as to whether he died in Ireland or in Tain, but in either case, his remains were buried in a specially built chape which in now in ruins but may still be visited. It is located with St Duthus Old Burial Ground, close to the Dornoch Firth.

St Duthac's Chapel soon became a place of sanctuary and pilgrimage, being visited by Robert the Bruce, but it was destroyed by fire in 1427 during fighting between members of clan Mackay and clan Ross, after which the relics of St Duthac were removed to St Duthac's Collegiate Church, which dates from 1360. There, King James IV (1473-1513) visited it annually from 1492 until his death at the Battle of Flodden in Northumberland, and the burgh developed into an important trading centre. However, the remains of the patron saint of Tain disappeared in 1560 during the Reformation.

St Duthac's Church is now at the centre of the excellent 'Tain through Time' project (✆+44 (0)1862 894089 ⌗tainmuseum.org. uk) which comprises three buildings around the churchyard. The ground floor of The Pilgrimage building in Tower Street features interpretive boards, murals and replica artefacts to tell the story of the pilgrims who made their way to Tain, while the town's heritage up to the Reformation is explored through paintings, calligraphic text and an accompanying soundtrack in the Town Loft.

A personal CD tour is available to guide visitors around the church itself, and continues to take in other significant buildings in the town for those who wish to venture further. The third and final 'Tain through Time' building is the 1960s-built Tain and District Museum on Caste Brae, which is home to a fascinating collection of objects, photographs and archives, and also houses a shop, retailing history books, Scottish music and souvenirs.

Apart from 'Tain in Time,' a key feature of the town is its centrally-

located tolbooth, which dates from the early years of the 18th century. It replaced a 1630 structure which served as court offices and a jail, as well as a place for the payment of taxes and tolls.

In 1656, troops commanded by Oliver Cromwell were quartered in Tain, and damaged many properties in the burgh, including the tolbooth. Worse was to follow, as famine and fire completed Cromwell's work, meaning that by the turn of the century little was left intact. A major fundraising appeal bankrolled the construction of the current tolbooth, and its tower houses the bell from its predecessor, cast in Flanders during 1630.

GLENMORANGIE DISTILLERY

⌂ Tain, Ross-shire IV19 1PZ ✆ +44 (0) 01862 892477 🖉 glenmorangie.com Travelling on the A9 it is impossible to miss Glenmorangie distillery, as it is accessed directly from the road, shortly after its junction with the B9174 from Tain.

Three tour options are available, with the popular Original Tour providing the chance to explore the distillery and sample a dram of Glenmorangie single malt.

The Signet Tour also includes a distillery visit, plus the chance to discover Glenmorangie Signet, "inspired by the aroma of a cup of coffee. Breathe in the espresso notes of Signet's chocolate malt barley and delve deeper into its secrets. Sip on our signature whisky, The Original, and a select Limited Edition, then enjoy Signet with a chocolate pairing."

The Heritage Tour follows a tour with a trip to the distillery's water source, the Tarlogie springs, and lunch in nearby Glenmorangie House.

Glenmorangie distillery was developed between 1843 and 1849, when the first spirit flowed. Its founder was William Mathieson, who utilised existing elements of the defunct Morangie Brewery, and in 1887 The Glenmorangie Distillery Co Ltd was formed. The plant was entirely rebuilt at that time, and Glenmorangie became one of the very first distilleries in Scotland to use steam to heat its stills rather than coal.

Macdonald & Muir Ltd, owners of the Highland Queen blended whisky brand, took a majority share in Glenmorangie during 1918, and the distillery went on to survive a period of silence in the mid-1930s. The more recent history of Glenmorangie has been notably

◀ *Glenmorangie distillery with the tallest stills in Scotland.*

SCOTCH
WHISKY

There are 2.2 million visits to Scotch Whisky distilleries a year, making the industry the second most popular tourist attraction in Scotland

VISIT www.scotch-whisky.org.uk

The USA has its Bourbons and ryes, Ireland has its whiskey (spelt with an 'e'), but for many people all over the world, Scotch is the true whisky. Following the A9 is an ideal way to learn all about this most fascinating of spirits, its heritage and its stylistic variety, as some 20 whisky distilleries are located within 10 miles of the Great Road North.

Debate still rages over which nation was the first to distil the amber nectar, with some (mainly Irish) sources claiming the honour for the Emerald Isle, while others (mainly Scots) insist that they discovered the art of whisky-making. Whatever the truth, the first written reference to Scotch whisky (as 'aqua vitae' – Latin for 'water of life') appears in an Exchequer Roll (a record of royal income and expenditure) of 1st June 1494.

The Latin translation states that "And by payment made to brother John Cor by precept of the comptroller, as he asserts, by the King's command to make aqua vitae within the period of the account, eight bolls of malt."

The origins of whisky lay in monastic establishments, where it was used both for medicinal purposes and for its pleasurable effects. Eight bolls of malt would have produced approximately 1,500 bottles of whisky, so it seems pretty certain that distilling was taking place on a significant scale well before that key date.

Whisky spread from its religious roots into the wider community, and by the 18th century, distilling was a well-established industry in Scotland, growing larger and more commercial as time went by. The creation of blended whisky (see below) during the mid-19th century led to it becoming a true drink for the world, being exported to countries all around the globe. The last few decades have also seen a great revival of interest in single malt Scotch (see below), and since 2000, more than 30 new distilleries have been established, from the Scottish Borders to the furthermost isles.

Scotch whisky's continuing success can be judged by the following facts and figures:

- 42 bottles (70cl @40% ABV) of Scotch whisky are shipped from Scotland to 175 markets around the world each second, totalling over 1.3bn every year
- Laid end to end those bottles would stretch about 350,000kms - that's 90% of the distance to the moon!
- Scotch Whisky exports are worth £4.9b
- In 2019, Scotch whisky accounted for 75% of Scottish food and drink exports, 21% of all UK food and drink exports, and 1.4% of all UK goods exports
- The Scotch whisky industry provides £5.5bn in gross value added (GVA) to the UK economy
- More than 10,000 people are directly employed in the Scotch whisky industry in Scotland and over 40,000 jobs across the UK are supported by the industry
- 7,000 of these jobs in rural areas of Scotland providing vital employment and investment to communities across the Highlands and Islands
- Around 90% of barley requirements of the industry are sourced in Scotland
- There are 2.2 million visits to Scotch Whisky distilleries a year, making the industry the second most popular tourist attraction in Scotland
- To be called Scotch whisky, the spirit must mature in oak casks in Scotland for at least 3 years
- There are currently 133 operating

SCOTCH WHISKY AND SOME DEFINITIONS

SINGLE MALT SCOTCH WHISKY

By law, a single malt whisky must be the product of just one distillery, though many different casks of varying ages may be mixed together for any particular bottling. The whisky has to be made from malted barley in pot stills, have a strength of 40% or higher, and be aged in oak casks for a minimum of three years.

SINGLE GRAIN SCOTCH WHISKY

Grain Scotch whisky is made from a small proportion of malted barley along with wheat or maize, and distillation takes place in large 'column' or 'continuous stills,' rather than the copper pot stills of malt whisky distilleries. Grain whisky is much cheaper to produce than single malt whisky, partly because the unmalted cereals are less expensive than malted barley, and partly because of the continuous and large-scale nature of the process. A proportion of grain whisky is mixed with single malt whisky to create blended Scotch, though single grain whiskies are also sometimes bottled.

BLENDED SCOTCH WHISKY

Although sales of malt Scotch whisky are increasing, blended spirit still accounts for more than 90 per cent of all Scotch whisky consumed around the world. Blending is one of the most skilful aspects of whisky production, and the best blenders are very highly regarded. They work almost exclusively by nose, rarely actually drinking any of the whiskies they are evaluating. The average blended whisky comprises malts from up to 30 different distilleries, along with two or three grain whiskies, and the blender will choose these to produce a whisky in the required style and at the required cost. More expensive blends will usually contain a higher proportion of malts and older whiskies than cheaper ones.

BLENDED MALT SCOTCH WHISKY

Blended malts represent a small but important sector of the Scotch whisky market. Previously referred to as 'vatted malts,' they consist of a number of different malt whiskies blended together. As with blended whiskies, any age statement on the bottle must refer to the youngest whisky in the blend.

MAKING MALT SCOTCH WHISKY

The process of producing malt whisky has, in essence, changed little through the centuries, although in recent years, greater automation and computerisation in many distilleries has reduced the level of individual skill and experience required by the operators.

Despite any amount of automation, however, the fact remains that the 'make' of no two distilleries is ever the same. While it is possible to copy production methods and equipment, use the same water source, barley and yeast, and mature spirit for the same duration in the same type of casks within apparently identical micro-climates, the result will always be distinctly different spirits.

By law, Scotch malt whisky must be distilled entirely from a mash of malted barley, and the business of making malt whisky begins by malting barley in order to induce germination. In traditional distillery-based floor maltings, the barley is steeped in water for two or three days, then spread on a malting floor, where rootlets develop as germination begins. So that the malt retains the sugars essential for fermentation, the partially germinated 'green malt', as it is known, is transferred to a kiln for around seven days and dried over a fire or by jets of hot air, sometimes with a quantity of peat used in the furnace to create a smokier style of whisky.

Today, only a handful of distilleries still malt their own barley, with the vast majority buying in malt prepared to their specification by commercial maltsters in large, automated plants.

Once dried, the malt is ground in a mill to produce 'grist,' after which the process of mashing begins. The grist is mixed with hot water in a large vessel known as a mash tun to extract fermentable sugars, and the sweet liquid that results from mashing is known as 'wort.' The 'draff,' which is left behind is high in protein, and makes excellent cattle feed.

The wort is pumped from the mash tun into a number of washbacks, traditionally made from Oregon pine or larch wood, but now frequently constructed of stainless steel. There yeast is added to promote fermentation and create alcohol. The end product of fermentation is a liquor known as 'wash,' which is transferred to copper pot wash stills, where it is brought to the boil.

Alcohol boils at a lower temperature than water, so the alcohol vapours rise from the still first and are condensed into liquid when they pass through coiled copper pipes or 'worms', immersed in vast wooden vats, or more modern 'shell and tube' condensers.

The alcohol produced must be re-distilled in order to obtain the purest 'cut' of spirit that will mature into whisky, and this takes place in vessels known as spirit stills. Pot stills vary greatly in size, shape and technical design, and this diversity is one of the variables that contribute to the style of spirit made.

The product of the spirit stills is referred to as 'new make,' and this clear liquid is reduced with water from its natural strength to around 63 or 64 per cent alcohol by volume before filling it to cask, as this is usually considered the optimum maturation strength.

Casks that previously held bourbon or sherry are the most popular for ageing whisky, and some distillers believe that up to 75 per cent of the character of the spirit is derived from maturation. The size of cask, as well as its previous contents, is yet another major variable of malt whisky production.

positive, with the complement of stills being doubled from two to four during a reconstruction programme in 1979, while capacity was again doubled a decade later with the installation of four more stills.

In 2004 Glenmorangie plc, as it had now become, was bought by Louis Vuitton Moet Hennessy (LVMH) for £300 million, and today Glenmorangie is the fourth-best-selling single malt in the world. Another expansion project was completed during 2008/9, when £4.5 million was spent on the installation of a supplementary mash tun, four new washbacks and four more stills. This development increased potential capacity from four million litres per year to six million litres. In 2021, the 'Lighthouse' distillery was opened alongside the main Glenmorangie production buildings. It comprises an eye-catching new stillhouse, complete with one pair of versatile stills and mashing and fermentation vessels, and is intended to operate as an experimental facility.

The Glenmorangie stills are the tallest pot stills in Scotland and are based on the design of the original ex-gin stills from London, installed when the distillery was founded. Their design contributes significantly to the light, sweet, fruity, floral character of Glenmorangie

The core range of single malts comprises Original (10-year-old), 18 and Signet, along with Quinta Ruban (port cask finish), Lasanta (sherry cask finish) and Nectar d'Or (sauternes cask finish). The distillery is also notable for its many limited-edition releases.

BALBLAIR DISTILLERY

Edderton, Tain, Ross-shire IV19 1LB ✆ + 44 (0) 1862 821273
balblair.com

Balblair distillery is located five miles north-west of Glenmorangie distillery, via the A836 off the roundabout on the A9 approaching the Dornoch Firth Bridge. The distillery boasts a stylish visitor centre and shop, and tours include access to one of the warehouses, sampling of several drams in the tasting room, and the chance to hand-bottle an exclusive expression from the cask.

1790 is given as the year in which the distillery was founded, making it one of the oldest surviving whisky-making plants in Scotland. In reality, however, the present distillery actually dates from the 1890s, with the 1790 original being located half a mile away.

That original was the work of John Ross of Balblair Farm, and the distillery remained in the Ross family until 1894, with major rebuilding taking place in 1872. Despite that programme of reconstruction, when Inverness wine merchant Alexander Cowan took on the lease of Balblair distillery from its owners the Balnagowan Estate, the plant was relocated to its present site during ˋ1894/95. The move was made in order to take advantage of the adjacent Inverness-Wick/Thurso railway line, facilitating the import of raw materials and the export of casks of whisky.

Balblair was silent from 1915 until 1947, when Keith solicitor Robert 'Bertie' Cumming purchased it for £48,000, recommencing distilling two years later after investing significantly in upgrading the distillery and increasing output. However, the distillery remains equipped with just a single pair of stills. When Cumming retired in 1970, he sold Balblair to the Canadian distiller Hiram Walker & Sons Ltd. Hiram Walker merged with Allied Vintners to become Allied Distillers in 1988, and Allied sold Balblair to Inver House eight years later. Today, Inver House is owned by Thai Beverages plc.

Balblair distillery plays a major part in the action of the 2012 Ken Loach film The Angels' Share, as the venue for the auctioning of a rare cask of Malt Mill whisky, and the pilfering of a quantity of said Malt Mill by the film's youthful Glaswegian protagonists who met as members of a community payback group.

Having long been notable for offering vintage expressions, each distilled in a single year and labelled as such, Balblair adopted a policy of releasing bottlings carrying age statements in 2019. The current Balblair single malt range comprises 12, 15, 18 and 25-year-old expressions, and the house style is medium-bodied, elegant, fruity, nutty and spicy.

DORNOCH

Until the construction of the Dornoch Firth bridge in 1991, the A9 route north ran west along the southern shore of the Dornoch Firth to Bonar Bridge (IV24 3EA), where it crossed the Kyle of Sutherland. The first bridge was built to the design of Thomas Telford in 1812, though the present structure dates from 1973. From Bonar Bridge, the 'old' A9 ran east again to join the modern A9 at Clashmore, north of the Dornoch Firth Bridge. Installing the new crossing cut more than 20 miles off the journey between Inverness and Thurso.

South of the A949 from Bonar Bridge to Clashmore is Skibo Castle (IV25 3RQ), but unless you happen to be one of the 400 elite global businessmen who are members of the ultra-exclusive Carnegie Club, you will not be allowed in.

Skibo Castle dates back to 1212 and was originally a residence for the Bishop of Caithness, but is best known as the Scottish home of Dunfermline-born US industrialist and philanthropist Andrew Carnegie. He spent more than the equivalent of £20m in today's terms acquiring, improving and expanding the estate and remodelling the castle itself during the late 1890s. Carnegie died in 1919, but the castle remained in the family until 1982, after which it became an exclusive hotel, frequented by Hollywood stars, and it was the venue for the marriage of Madonna and Guy Ritchie in December 2000, an event attended by the likes of Gwyneth Paltrow, Donatella Versace and Sting.

A couple of miles north of the Dornoch Firth Bridge, the A949 branches east from the A9 and runs for just over two miles east to the historic town of Dornoch, located on the north shore of the Dornoch Firth, near to where it opens into the Moray Firth ⊘visitdornoch.com.

HISTORYLINKS MUSEUM

⌂The Meadows, Dornoch, Sutherland IV25 3SF ✆+44 (0) 1862 811275
⊘historylinks.org.uk

Historylinks is a great place to learn about Dornoch and its environs. It hosts displays that include Carnegie's life at Skibo Castle, the golf professional's workshop used by Donald Ross (see p.158), crofting and 'clearances' exhibits, and material relating to the Dornoch Light Railway, that ran from the main Inverness-Wick/Thurso line to Dornoch between 1902 and 1960. The existence of the railway, along with its golf course and beaches, helped to make Dornoch a popular holiday resort from the early 20th century. Historylinks Museum also boasts an excellent shop stocked with books, gifts, tartan and woollen items.

DORNOCH CATHEDRAL

⌂IV25 3SJ ⊘dornoch-cathedral.com
Now a Church of Scotland parish church, this former cathedral is still universally referred to by its former name. It was constructed during the 13th century, and in recent times gained fame as the

venue for the baptism of Madonna and Guy Richie's son Rocco in 2000.

The cathedral was built by the Bishop of Caithness, Gilbert de Moravia, who was elected to that position in 1222, and construction began soon after. Although it is not known exactly how long it took to build the cathedral, work was sufficiently completed for a service to be held there in 1239, six years before the death of Gilbert.

In 1570 the cathedral was almost totally destroyed by fire during a clan feud between the Murrays and Mackay, and Gilbert de Moravia's tomb was desecrated. Only the transept walls and chancel survived the blaze, and partial restoration was undertaken in 1616 by Sir Robert Gordon. The work was not completed for more than two centuries, with Elizabeth, Duchess-Countess of Sutherland funding it between 1835 and 1837, with a Sutherland burial vault being added.

DORNOCH DISTILLERY

✉ Castle Street, Dornoch, Sutherland IV253SD ✆ +44 (0) 1862 810637
⌖ thompsonbrothersdistillery.com

In 2000, the Thompson family acquired the historic Dornoch Castle, which had been operating as a hotel since 1947, though originally it was the bishop's palace. Under the Thompsons' control, the hotel began to develop a reputation for the selection of whiskies it offered, and Phil and Simon, sons of owners Colin and Ros, were eager to learn about Scotch and to develop the whisky selection on offer.

Not content with establishing one of the world's leading whisky bars in Dornoch, Phil and Simon Thompson developed a small-scale distillery in the castle's former fire station building during 2016. The building in question measures only 500 square feet, but the Thompsons have managed to fit in a mash tun, six oak washbacks, a pair of Portuguese whisky stills and a gin still.

Annual capacity of the distillery is around 30,000 litres, divided almost equally at present between gin and whisky production, and the Thompsons have a passion for 'old school' distilling, using floor-malted barley, sometimes heritage varieties, and practising very long fermentations. Their first limited edition, single malt whisky was released as a three-year-old in the autumn of 2020. Distillery tours are available.

▲ *Dornoch beach.*

ROYAL DORNOCH GOLF CLUB

✉Golf Rd, Dornoch IV25 3LW ✆+44 (0)1862 810219 🌐royaldornoch.com

One of the great attractions of this area is Royal Dornoch Golf Club, which draws players from all over the world, keen to compete on this coastal course. The sport has been played here since 1616, and the club was formed in 1877. The Championship Course is ranked fifth-best in the world, outside of the USA, and the club boasts the 18-hole Struie Course.

Back in 1877 Dornoch Town Council granted permission for the Sutherland Golfing Society to play on the town links, a move which ultimately boosted tourism in the area to a significant degree. A few years later, the course was attracting high-profile players, including Andrew Carnegie, then the world's richest man, and King Edward VII, who granted the club its 'royal' status in 1906.

Donald Ross, born in St Gilbert Street, Dornoch during 1872, served as a greenkeeper at the course before going on to become the most renowned golf course architect in the USA, designing hundreds of courses, while in 1907, his brother Alex won the prestigious US Open. Royal Dornoch was voted Scotland's Best Golf Course in 2020 in the World Golf Awards.

DORNOCH BEACH

If golf brought visitors to Dornoch, then another attraction was the excellent beach, with its dunes and miles of golden sands. The beach is located beside the golf course, and now accorded 'blue flag' status for its water quality, safety, and environmental awareness.

THE MOUND AND GOLSPIE

Between 1803 and 1821 Thomas Telford was responsible for the construction of 920 miles of road and more than 1200 bridges in the Highlands. One project he undertook in the north-east was the creation of a bridge at Loch Fleet, to replace the existing ferry service. That bridge is still in use, today, forming part of the A9.

Its construction was a major feat of engineering and involved a 1,000-yards-long earthen mound to carry a road bridge across the junction of Loch Fleet and the River Fleet Its four arches – now six – were equipped with sluice gates to hold back the tide as it rose and release fresh water from the river as the tide fell.

The earthwork created by Telford is still referred to as 'The Mound,' and the internationally important Loch Fleet Nature Reserve (⊘ naturescot.com) may be accessed on the south shore of the loch by a minor road through Skelbo, off the A9 (IV25 3QG is the nearest postcode), or on the north shore via a minor road from Golspie via Balblair Woods to Littleferry (✉ KW10 6TD is the nearest postcode.)

The Nature Reserve is based on the large tidal basin of Loch Fleet, with coastal heath, dunes and native Scots Pine woods. Otters, seals, wildfowl and seabirds are common sights, along with butterflies and orchids, while crested tits, Scottish crossbills and pine marten may be observed in the woodland areas. According to NatureScot, "Specialist species thrive in the pine forest, including twinflower and one-flowered wintergreen."

Having crossed The Mound, the A9 runs for 3.5 miles to the coastal village of Golspie, with its fine, sandy beaches, golf course and 16th century St Andrews Church. Golspie lies in the shadow of Ben Bhraggie, or Beinn a' Bhragaidh in Gaelic, which rises to just

▲ Dunrobin castle.

over 1,300 feet. It is home to a statue that was controversial long before the Black Lives Matter movement began its campaigns to remove statues considered offensive to modern sensibilities.

The statue in question is of George Granville Leveson-Gower, the first Duke of Sutherland, and comprises a 24-feet-high image of the duke, on a 76-feet-hgh pedestal. It was erected near the summit of Ben Bragghie in 1837, following the duke's death four years earlier.

George Granville Leveson-Gower was a millionaire who had twice served as a Member of Parliament during the 1780s and 1790s. He later became the British ambassador in Paris, and in 1785, he married Elizabeth, the Countess of Sutherland, in the process becoming the owner of a vast Highland estate – the largest in Europe at the time.

The reason for his subsequent notoriety, and attempts, both physical and political, to remove his statue was the role he played in the period known as the 'Highland Clearances.' The 'Clearances' took place during the early years of the 19th century, when tenant farmers were removed from their land and either resettled by the coast or forced to emigrate in order to make way for sheep – which yielded far greater profits for the landowners than their tenants ever could.

In defence of the Duke of Sutherland, he was horrified by the state of extreme poverty in which many of his tenants lived and believed that fishing rather than subsistence farming would offer them a better future. However, he was implicit in forced evictions of families, carried out by his ruthless factor Patrick Sellar, and this period of Highland history has cast a long shadow over the reputations of those involved.

DUNROBIN CASTLE

Golspie, Sutherland KW10 6SF + 44 (0) 1408 633177, dunrobincastle.co.uk

Dunrobin Castle is situated one mile north of Golspie off the A9, and five miles south of Brora. It is the most northerly of Scotland's 'great houses' and the largest in the Northern Highlands, with no fewer than 189 rooms.

As the ancestral home of the Dukes of Sutherland, the castle offers visitors fascinating insights into how the family lived in days gone by, and a tour embraces some of the castle's grand public rooms, including the splendid wood-panelled dining room and music room, drawing room complete with paintings by Canaletto and portraits by Reynolds and Hopner, the duke's study and magnificent library – home to more than 10,000 volumes. On a more domestic scale, are the seamstress's room, containing a collection of family robes, along with the nanny's room, nursery, and 'below stairs,' the footman's pantry.

Outside the castle, the gardens complement the flamboyant building perfectly, and are little changed since they were laid out 150 years ago by Sir Charles Barry. They include two parterres laid out around circular pools with fountains, inspired by the gardens of the Palace of Versailles.

A museum is also located in the formal castle grounds, and was originally built as a summer house by William, Earl of Sutherland, and extended by the 3rd Duke. The museum displays the heads of animals shot by members of the family while on safari, ethnographic items and important collections of archaeological relics and Pictish slabs and symbol stones.

Additionally, falconry displays are staged twice daily during the summer months on the castle lawn, with the resident falconer demonstrating the varied hunting methods used by owls, hawks and falcons in a series of aerobatic displays.

The castle's team room offers home-made snacks and meals, and the gift shop stocks a range of quality Scottish gift and craft items, plus much else besides.

Dunrobin castle has been home to the Sutherlands since the 13th century, with the earldom of Sutherland being created in 1235. The site is thought to be that previously occupied by a medieval fort. The original keep of the castle remains within the series of later extensions and alterations, meaning that Dunrobin is one of Scotland's oldest inhabited houses.

The castle's present appearance and layout is due to the work of Sir Charles Barry, the architect who designed the Houses of Parliament in London, and who undertook the project to turn Dunrobin from a fortress into a Scottish 'baronial-style' house in 1845. A strong French influence pervades the exterior of Dunrobin, with its conical spires, but Barry's interior was largely destroyed during a fire in 1915. Scottish architect Sir Robert Lorimer created a new interior and also made some external alterations.

Between 1965 and 1972 Dunrobin castle served as a boys' boarding school, before reverting to a family home for the earls of Sutherland.

CLYNELISH AND BRORA DISTILLERIES

⌂Brora, Sutherland KW9 6LR ✆+44 (0) 1408 623003 ⌖malts.com
Clynelish and Brora distilleries are accessed by a minor road to the west
of the A9, just north of Brora village.

The visitor offering at Clynelish has recently undergone a major
upgrade, with the distillery having been rebranded as 'The
Highland Home of Johnnie Walker.' A new bar and tasting area
offering views of the Sutherland coast has been constructed,
while Clynelish's long links with Johnnie Walker blended Scotch
are explored in an entertaining and accessible way. Distillery-
exclusive and fill-your-own bottling options are available.

Brora tours are strictly by appointment only, with a three three-
hours-long 'Brora Awakened Tour' and a four to five hours four and
five hours 'Eras of Brora Tour.' Lunch and exclusive tastings are
included in both options.

Clynelish is the northernmost distillery in Diageo's portfolio and
there are actually two distilleries on the Clynelish site, with the
original stone structures dating from 1819 standing alongside
their 1960s replacements.

The distillery was founded by the Marquess of Stafford, later 1st
Duke of Sutherland, and it not only benefitted from a supply of
locally-grown barley, but also abundant peat for firing the malt
kilns, while fuel was also provided by the local Brora coal mine,
which had been in use since the 16th century.

Clynelish had a number of owners before John Walker & Sons
Ltd bought into it during 1916, and Walker's duly became part of
the Distillers Company Ltd (DCL) in 1925. Within five years DCL
owned the entire share capital of Clynelish, subsequently moving
the distillery into the care of its Scottish Malt Distillers (SMD)
subsidiary.

During the 1960s, DCL expanded and rebuilt many of its existing
distilleries to cope with the increasing demand for blended
Scotch whisky, and in the case of Clynelish, an entirely new
modernistic plant was built during 1967/68 alongside the old
production buildings. The original distillery closed down in May
1968, but was revived the following year, being re-named Brora.
Between 1969 and 1973 Brora distilled relatively heavily-peated
spirit, with more batches being produced from time to time in
subsequent years, as DCL required additional stocks of Islay-style
spirit for blending purposes. Today, bottlings of peaty Brora have
achieved a cult status among connoisseurs.

▲ *Helmsdale village.*

Brora finally closed in 1983, but remained largely intact, with its quirky, tarnished pair of stills in place. Then, between 2017 and 2021, the distillery was revived, with the restored stills now gleaming brightly. 'Old style' Brora is being produced once more! The principal single malt on the market is named Triptych, and includes three bottles of single cask vintage Brora. However, the cost is £36,000.

Meanwhile, the 'new' Clynelish plant, with its six stills, provides comparatively large amounts of spirit for blending, and it was only in 2002 that a 14-year-old 'house' bottling of Clynelish was released. A wider selection of expressions is now available, some exclusive to the distillery, while the house style is floral, malty, fruity, spicy and oily, with hints of seaweed and smoke.

HELMSDALE

Some 11 miles north-east of Brora on the A9 is the fishing port of Helmsdale (helmsdale.org), which has its origins in Viking times, when a settlement was established at the mouth of the River Helmsdale. The present village was laid out in a grid pattern by the Sutherland Estates from 1814 onwards, with the aim of providing accommodation for some of the tenants 'cleared' from inland areas of Sutherland. The intention was for the cleared

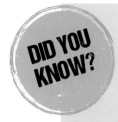

HRH Prince George, The Duke of Kent, younger brother of King Edward VIII and King George V, and an Air Commodore in the RAF, was the first member of a British Royal Family to die on active military service since the death of James IV of Scotland at the Battle of Flodden in 1513. He perished on 25th August 1942 when the Short Sunderland seaplane in which he was a passenger crashed into Eagle's Rock, near Berriedale, killing 14 of the 15 men on board. The site of the crash is marked with a Celtic cross memorial, and Berriedale is listed as the location where the duke died on his death certificate.

crofters to combine farming with fishing, and in particular herring fishing, as the 'silver darlings' were in plentiful supply around this time, and herring paid wages for many people during the 19th century along the east Sutherland and Caithness coasts.

Helmsdale harbour was built in 1818, extended in 1823 and again in 1892, with up to 200 fishing boars calling Helmsdale home during the herring 'boom.' Many of those 'cleared' tenants who did not find a home at Helmsdale had no choice but to emigrate to the USA or Australia, and an Emigrants Statue commemorating their ordeal is situated above the harbour, on the south bank of the river in Couper Park.

Sutherland seems an unlikely place to have experienced a 'gold rush,' but it did so during 1869, 20 years after the Californian gold rush on the other side of the Atlantic. A single gold nugget had been discovered in the River Helmsdale during 1818, and subsequently made into a ring, owned by the Sutherland family, but late in 1868, Robert Nelson Gilchrist, a native of the Strath of Kildonan, west of Helmsdale, discovered more gold when panning in the River Helmsdale.

The richest deposits were in the Suisgill and Kildonan burns, and during the first half of 1869, some 600 would-be prospectors arrived in the area, establishing a shanty town known in Gaelic as Baile an Or - Village of the Gold - located close to the present day A897. Gold was indeed discovered, but not enough to make anyone rich, and the Duke of Sutherland ended the 'rush' by ceasing to licence prospectors at the end of 1869.

The story of the Kildonan Gold Rush is told in Timespan Heritage and Arts Centre (✉Dunrobin Street, Helmsdale, Sutherland KW8 6JA ✆+44 (0) 1431 821327 ⌚imespan.org.uk) a museum of social and natural history, contemporary art gallery, archive, gift shop, herb garden and cafe.

Timespan combines local folklore and tales with a collection of objects spanning several thousand years, while a virtual reality room recreates the local township of Caen as it was two centuries ago. The room also hosts five animated films relating to the area's myths, legends and superstitions. Elsewhere, there are recreations of a croft, byre, smithy, and a shop as they would have been 150 years ago. Audio tours are available, while quizzes and puzzles and much more will keep younger visitors entertained.

ORD OF CAITHNESS, BADBEA AND BERRIEDALE

Two miles north of Helmsdale is the mighty Ord of Caithness, the boundary between the counties of Sutherland and Caithness, and historically a daunting passage to the far north (⌚caithnessandsutherland.com/⌚caithness.org).

According to Francis Groom (Ordnance Gazetteer of Scotland -1882-4) the Ord of Caithness was "...an abrupt, broad, lofty, granite mountain overhanging the sea...The old road over it, formerly the only land ingress to Caithness, traversed the crest of its stupendous seaward precipices at a height and in a manner most appalling to both man and beast; and even the present road, formed in 1811, rises to an elevation of 726 feet above sea-level, and has very stiff gradients. ..."

Little wonder that historically the most popular route into Caithness was by way of the sea rather than the land!

In recent years, the A9 road over the Ord has been upgraded to improve overtaking opportunities, but it is still obvious to the modern traveller how formidable a barrier the Ord once presented.

A fascinating feature just off the A9 after the Ord has been conquered is the 'clearance village' of Badbea. People cleared from more fertile land away from the coast to make way for sheep moved here and began to construct houses and create crofts from 1792 onwards.

Each crofter rented land and reared livestock and grew vegetables, with many also being involved with herring fishing, while illicit whisky stills were not unknown. Badbea stretched for just over a mile of precipitous hillside to the east of what is now the A9, and it is said that children and livestock had to be tethered to rocks when gales blew along this exposed stretch of coast.

With the decline of herring fishing in the later years of the 19th century, the population of Badbea fell, with some residents emigrating to Australia, New Zealand and North America, and by the 1870s, just six working crofts remained. The village was finally abandoned in 1911, and today the remains of croft houses and field walls tell a poignant tale of the 60 to 100 hardy souls who once called this home.

A monument was erected in 1911 by David M Sutherland, son of former Badbea resident Alexander Robert Sutherland, who emigrated to New Zealand in 1839, to 'Commemorate the people of Badbea.'

Beyond Badbea, the A9 drops steeply to a bridge over the Berriedale Water at Berriedale Braes, before climbing again through a series of bends, though the most severe hairpin was removed during a £9.6m realignment scheme that opened during the summer of 2020. Before that, it was frequently necessary for vehicles to stop on the bend's approach to allow for an oncoming HGV to negotiate the sharp turn.

When the Inverness to Wick railway was constructed during the 1860s and '70s, the impossibility of bridging the Berriedale Braes meant that the line instead ran inland from Helmsdale, via Kinbrace and Forsinard, before heading east to the coast and Wick from Georgemas Junction.

DUNBEATH

The fishing village of Dunbeath is located six miles north of Berriedale, and the modern A9 crosses the Dunbeath Water on a bridge built in 1989 to bypass Dunbeath itself. The settlement dates from the 'herring boom' years of the early 19th century and its harbour was once home to 100 fishing boats.

The village was also the birthplace of Neil Miller Gunn (1891-1973), a prominent Scottish nationalist and one of the country's finest novelists. His life and work are celebrated in:

DUNBEATH HERITAGE CENTRE

⌂The Old School, Dunbeath, Caithness KW6 6ED ✆+44 (0) 1593 731233
⌕dunbeath-heritage.org.uk.

The Centre is described as offering 'A Journey Through the Past,
Places and People of Dunbeath; their stories and history, a hub for
the arts, culture and the work of Neil Gunn."
  Many of Gunn's novels are set on his native Caithness coast, most
notably his epic historical novel centred around the herring fishing
bonanza of the early 19th century, The Silver Darlings, and his
best-known work Highland River (1937). In Highland River the central
protagonist Kenn follows the strath inland from Dunbeath to the
source of the Dunbeath Water.
  A statue on Dunbeath harbourside references an episode
from the novel, depicting 'Kenn and the Salmon.' The harbour
also provides the best view of the privately-owned Dunbeath
Castle, perched on the cliffs to the south of the village. The
original castle was constructed during the 15th century, but the
present structure dates mainly from the 17th century, with later
extensions.

*"All the county on this side, from Dunbeth [sic] to the extremity, is
flat, or at lest very seldom interrupted with hills, and those low; but
the coasts rocky, and composed of stupendous cliffs"*
Thomas Pennant, A Tour in Scotland 1769 (London: Benjamin White, 1776)

THE LAIDHAY CROFT MUSEUM

Dunbeath, Caithness ⌂KW6 6EH✆+44 (0) 1593 731270 ⌕laidhay.co.uk
The museum is situated beside the A9, just north of Dunbeath,
and this restored 200-year-old rush-thatched longhouse provides
a fascinating insight into the life of a crofting family in times gone
by. The actual croft-house is furnished and equipped as it might
have been at the turn of the 19th century, and the adjoining byre
contains a fine collection of original crofting implements. There is
also a tearoom, offering a range of drinks and homemade cakes.
  Two miles north-east of Laidhay, and just east of the A9 is
Latheronwheel, a small village with a picturesque harbour,
well worth taking the time to visit. Latheronwheel was a
planned settlement, established in 1835, with the harbour being
constructed some five years later. Early salmon fishing here was

superseded by the search for herring, and at one time, around 50 commercial fishing vessels operated from Latheronwheel.

Climbing the safe cliffs around the harbour provides great views south along the rocky Caithness coast, and the nearby Fairy Glen – complete with tiny fairy house, all created and maintained by local volunteers, is a must-see for all age groups.

A mile beyond Latheronwheel, the A9 arrives at the scattered village of Latheron, where it takes a turn inland towards Thurso.

DETOUR VIA WICK AND JOHN O'GROATS

It is here that you can make a longer detour via Wick and John O'Groats and you can see full details of what to visit from page 174 onwards

THURSO

Until 1997, the A9 carried on north from Latheron to Wick and Thurso via John O'Groats, with the inland road to Thurso being numbered the A895. On 16th May of that year, however, the A895 was re-designated the A9, reflecting the increasing importance of the route to Orkney via Thurso and the port of Scrabster. The route from Latheron to John O'Groats then became the A99.

From Latheron, the modern A9 crosses the bleak moorland of Causeymire, passing Loch Rangag and running for 17 miles to Georgemas Junction. Here, the A9 meets the A882 from Wick, and close by is where the Far North line from Inverness splits between branches to Wick
and Thurso.

North of Georgemas, the A9 reaches Thurso (✉ discoverthurso. co.uk) after six miles. Located on the north coast of Caithness, Thurso has the distinction of being Scotland's most northerly mainland town, complete with the country's most northerly railway station.

Thurso's origins date back to at least 900, when the Vikings used the mouth of the River Thurso as a harbour for trade and fishing, and during subsequent centuries the town developed in what is now known as Old Thurso, where the ruins of Old St Peter's Church are located. The earliest part of the church dates from the early 12th century. The 'new town' was established from 1798 onwards by local landowner Sir John Sinclair of Ulbster, using a grid system, still apparent today.

▲ *In the filling station at Wolfburn distillery.*

During the 1950s the population of Thurso swelled significantly with an influx of people employed at Dounreay Nuclear Power Development Establishment, located on a former airfield eight miles west of the town. The incomers were known by locals as 'The Atomics,' and by the 1970s, some 3,500 staff were on the Dounreay payroll. The last reactor at Dounreay closed down in 1994 but long-term decommissioning of the site still employs significant numbers.

Today, Thurso is best-known by visitors for its proximity to Scrabster, a mile and a half to the north-west, and the mainland terminal for car ferry services to the Orkney Islands. It is also a somewhat unlikely mecca for surfers from all over the world, with the prime surfing season being between October and April. Looking out across Thurso Bay, the Orkney Island of Hoy with its distinctive red sandstone cliffs is visible in the distance.

WOLFBURN DISTILLERY

⌂ Henderson Park, Thurso, Caithness KW14 7XW   ✆ + 44 (0) 1847 891051
🖰 wolfburn.com

Until the opening of 8 Doors in John O'Groats during 2022, Wolfburn was the most northerly malt distillery in mainland Scotland, producing a single malt that is beginning to make it mark alongside much longer-established competitors.

Wolfburn is a no-frills distillery, built in a business park on the outskirts of Thurso. There is no formal visitor centre, but highly informative tours focus on the nitty-gritty of whisky-making. There are opportunities to try several drams from the Wolfburn range and also buy bottles and branded merchandise. There are three tours each weekday, and booking is essential.

Wolfburn is one of Scotland's younger distilleries, having been commissioned during the first few weeks of 2013. The new facility is actually the second Wolfburn distillery, with the original operating between 1821 and the 1850s in the hands of the Smith family. Tax records from the early 19th century reveal that Wolfburn was once the largest distillery in Caithness, turning out some 125,000 litres of spirit during 1826.

The second Wolfburn distillery is situated just a few yards from the first, and draws its water from the same source, namely the Wolf Burn. The site comprises the production buildings and two warehouses, and one pair of stills is in situ, capable of producing up to 135,000 litres per year. All ageing and bottling take place on site, and spirit is filled into ex-Bourbon quarter casks, ex-Bourbon hogsheads, barrels and sherry butts.

Most of the output is unpeated, but some lightly peated spirit has been produced since 2014, and the first single malt release came in 2016. Today, there is quite a range on offer, including Northland, matured in American oak quarter casks, Aurora, aged in a combination of ex-Bourbon and oloroso sherry casks, the lightly-peated Morven, and the 58%abv Langskip, matured entirely in first-fill Bourbon casks. Additionally, Wolfburn has an energetic programme of limited-edition releases.

The use of clear worts produced during the mashing process and long fermentations in the four stainless steel leads to a 'house style' that is fruity, malty, and sweet, with floral hints on the nose.

NORTH POINT DISTILLERY

✉ Murkle House, Forss Business and Energy Park, Forss KW14 7UZ ✆ +44 (0) 1847 808120 🔗 northpointdistillery.com

North Point distillery is located six miles west of Thurso and produces North Point Pilot Rum and Spiced Rum, along with Crosskirk Bay Gin and Burgh Island London Dry Gin. Rum is made using sustainably sourced sugarcane and molasses from the Caribbean, and whisky casks are employed to mature and finish the spirit.

 Scrabster harbour.

Distillation takes place in an electronically-powered still named Sandy Stroma, equipped with a whisky 'helmet,' a brandy and rum column, and a botanical gin basket. A Copper Distillery Tour with tasting of core range spirits is available.

SCRABSTER

scrabster.co.uk

Scrabster Harbour is marketed to the public as "your gateway to the north," and is situated a mile and a half north-west of Thurso at the western end of Thurso Bay, sheltered by the cliffs of Holborn Head. It is an excellent natural harbour, and not surprisingly, its use dates back a very long way, in fact, all the way back to the Vikings. It features in The Orkneying Saga, written c.1225, where it is named in Old Norse as Skarabolstadr.

Despite its long history, the first formal pier was not constructed at Scrabster until the 1820s, when Thomas Telford created one, along with a road linking the harbour to Thurso. Further harbour developments went on over the succeeding decades, and by 1856, Scrabster had assumed its present role as the principal terminal for travel to the Orkney Islands, also hosting steam vessels bound for Aberdeen and Glasgow.

In 1862, Holborn Head lighthouse was built close to the harbour, and a dozen years later, the Highland Railway line was extended to Thurso, with horse-drawn buses ferrying passengers between the station and harbour. During the 19th century, flagstone quarrying was a major industry in Caithness, and as the most important port in the far north, Scrabster harbour played a significant role in the trade.

During the second half of the 20th century, increased car ownership and the growth of tourism in Scotland led to the installation of roll-on-roll-off vehicle ferry facilities and a dedicated terminus for public use during the 1970s. The crossing runs from Thurso across the frequently turbulent Pentland Firth, noted for its strong tides, and docks at the ancient Orkney port of Stromness. Ferry services to the Faroe Islands and Iceland from Thurso also operated for some time.

Scrabster has long played a crucial role in the Scottish fishing industry, and facilities for fishermen and other users have been expanded and improved over the years. Scrabster Harbour Trust has spent £35 million since 2001 on harbour facilities, as part of an ongoing total investment of £50 million.

Some 1,000 fishing vessels use the port each year, with landings being valued at more than £20 million. The catch includes whitefish and shellfish, including brown crab, lobsters, prawns and scallops. Much of it is landed by boats of diverse nationalities, and is transported from Scrabster in refrigerated trucks to markets as far away as Spain.

In addition to fishing and ferry vessels, cruise ships have become regular visitors to Scrabster in recent years, and the port is also used by operators in the oil, gas and renewables sectors.

DETOUR

Once you have reached the north coast of mainland Scotland you can then make a decsion whether to catch a ferry to Orkney from Scrabster to Stromness ⊘ northlinkferries.co.uk or Gills Bay to St Margaret's Hope ⊘ pentlandferries.co.uk

Latheron to Wick, John O'Groats and Thurso

Just past the A9 junction with the A99 at Latheron is

CLANN GUNN HERITAGE CENTRE & MUSEUM

⌂Latheron, Caithness KW5 6DN ✆+44 (0) 1593 528798
⌂clangunnociety.org

The centre is housed in the Old Latheron Parish Church, which dates from the 18th century, and is operated by the Clan Gunn Society. Clan Gunn claims direct descent from the Norse Jarls – or earls – of Orkney. The Centre contains one of the best clan archives in Scotland and has a shop selling Clan Gunn tartan souvenirs and books.

LYBSTER

The village of Lybster is located some four miles north-east of Latheron, and the first fishing activity began there during the 1790s, focusing on lobsters. So plentiful were the catches that in 1810 the local laird, General Patrick Sinclair constructed a wooden pier at the mouth of the Reisgill Burn so that his tenants could capitalise on the bounty of the sea.

During 1833 this was replaced by a large, stone-built harbour, with the pier being widened in 1849. By that date, Lyster was the third-largest herring fishing station in Scotland, after only Wick and Fraserburgh, with more than 100 vessels using the harbour. However, the herring trade had declined significantly by the 1890s, and Lybster was soon a shadow of its former self.

Today, the harbour is still active, with a number of inshore fishing vessels based there, fishing principally for crab, lobster and prawns. Its location is notably attractive, being situated below steep, grassy cliffs which provide it with invaluable shelter.

For many years, the range of stone-built, harbour-side buildings where fishermen stored their gear lay derelict, but these have now been restored and are home to:

THE WATERLINES HERITAGE CENTRE

⌂Lybster KW3 6DB ✆+44 (0) 1593 721520

The centre celebrates Lybster's fishing heritage with a range of displays and exhibits, not to mention a shop and café.

In 2019, Lybster stood in for a Falklands Islands port during filming of an episode of the Netflix drama The Crown.

GREY CAIRNS OF CAMSTER

historicenvirnoment.scot

A pair of Neolithic tombs, located five miles along an unclassified road, which joins the A99 five miles north of Lybster. They were built more than 5,000 years ago and according to Historic Environment Scotland, The Long Cairn "...has a long history of exploration, and prior to the first excavations in 1865–6 it had a very different profile... Before excavation, it had the appearance of a series of humps joined by a spine...Two burial chambers were found in the cairn. Both had originally formed part of separate round cairns, entered by cramped passages. Later, it seems, they were incorporated into the single long cairn we see today, though nobody is sure why. The development of the cairn and its original appearance are still disputed."

In terms of the Round Cairn, "Excavations in the 1800s found burnt human remains, flint tools and pottery. Its passage had been deliberately blocked, and inside two skeletons were found, apparently placed in a sitting position."

Two of the oldest stone monuments in Scotland, the Grey Cairns of Camster provide a fascinating insight into Neolithic funerary practices.

WHALIGOE STEPS

Ulbster KW2 6AB

The steps are located on the coast some seven miles north-east of Lybster and are a remarkable survivor of the days when herring fishing was a major industry in Caithness.

No fewer than 365 flagstone steps connect the primitive harbour with the village 250 feet above in a zigzagging pattern. The steps were in place when Thomas Pennant visited during 1769, but the present configuration is thought to date from 1792.

The area known as 'The Bink' is home to remains of a salt store – used to cure herrings, and a winch, for hoisting boats out of the often-inhospitable waters of Whaligoe Haven. By 1850, no fewer than 50 boats were based at Whaligoe during the summer herring fishing season, and fisherwomen faced the daunting task of carrying baskets of fish up the 365 steps before a seven-miles walk to the fish market in Wick.

▲ Whaligoe steps.

"In this parish [Wick] there is a haven for fishing boats, called Whaligo, [sic] which is a creek betwixt two high rocks. Though the height of one of these rocks is surprizing, yet the country people have made steps by which they go up and down, carrying heavy burdens on their back; which a stranger, without seeing, would scarcely believe. This is a fine fishing coast"
Thomas Pennant, A Tour in Scotland 1769 (London: Benjamin White, 1776)

WICK

The town was first settled in Norse times and is mentioned in a saga dating from 1140. Until the latter years of the 18th century, it was little more than a modest fishing village, but in 1767 a number of local merchants kitted out two boats to fish for herring, and soon achieved great success.

Local Member of Parliament Sir John Sinclair saw that herring could provide real prosperity for the area, and he arranged for several Dutch fishermen to spend time in Wick teaching the resident fishermen how to catch and process herring.

By 1800, in excess of 200 boats were fishing out of Wick during the summer herring season, and in 1808 the British Fisheries Society enlarged the harbour, and a model fishing village was

▲ *Wick harbour.*

created, being named Pulteneytown after British Fisheries
Society director Sir William Pulteney. As with so much other
infrastructure in the Highlands, the new harbour was designed by
Thomas Telford and it opened in 1810, though so successful was it
that 14 years later further extension was required.

The height of Wick's 'herring boom' popularity came in the year
1862, when no fewer than 1,122 vessels were based there, along
with 3,800 fishermen and 4,000 curers. Not surprisingly, there
was often something of a 'Wild West' frontier town feel about
Wick, and drunkenness and fighting were common.

The local contributor to the New Statistical Account of 1845
wrote that "There is great consumption of spirits, there being
22 public houses in Wick, and 23 in Pulteneytown...Seminaries
of Satan and Belial." It has been estimated that in excess of 800
gallons of whisky – or some 5,000 bottles – were being consumed
each week!

As a result of the effects of this excessive drinking, Wick was
one of few places outside the USA to impose prohibition, and
between 28th May 1922 and 28th May 1947, there were no public
houses or licensed grocers in the town open for the sale of
alcohol to the public. Prohibition lasted eleven years longer in
Wick than it did in the USA.

A great place to explore the often-tumultuous history of Wick and herring fishing is the Wick Heritage Museum ⌂20 Bank Row, Wick KW1 5EY ✆+44 (0) 1955 605393 🖝wickheritage.org). The Museum is home to the Wick Society, and features a fascinating range of displays relating to Wick and its environs, including a number of fully furnished household rooms portraying past life and times.

There is a particular emphasis on the fishing industry, with displays including a fishing hall, cooperage and kippering kiln, not to mention the 'head' of the lighthouse formerly located at Noss Head, just north of Wick, transferred in the museum after the lighthouse was automated in 1987.

The museum also has possession of the old lifeboat shed, now home to the Isabella Fortuna, a rare surviving traditional 'Fifie' fishing vessel, restored to her former glory and a majestic sight when in full sail.

One of the great treasures of the museum is The Johnston Collection, which represents the work of three generations of Caithness photographers who captured images of life in and around the area between 1863 and 1975. During that period, they produced some 100,000 glass plate negatives, of which half survive and are held by the Wick Society. The Johnston Collection has its own website (🖝johnstoncollection.net), complete with a searchable database.

THE CASTLES OF OLD WICK, SINCLAIR AND GIRNIGOE

⌂KW1 5TJ 🖝historicenvironment.scot

The castleof Old Wick is signposted from the town centre and is one of the most striking medieval sites in the far north. Dramatically situated on a narrow promontory, with towering cliffs on three sides, the castle is locally known as 'The Old Man of Wick.' Although significantly ruined, part of a four-storey tower remains, and the structure is thought to date from the 14th century, or later, although it was certainly in existence during the 16th century, when it was besieged by members of the Sinclair clan, who were feuding with its Sutherland owners.

Two other ruined castles of note with a strong Sinclair connection are located close to Wick, namely Castles Sinclair and Girnigoe (⌂KW1 4QT 🖝hisotricenvironment.scot). The pair of fortresses are 4.5 miles north of Wick, via Staxigoe, and stand on a narrow, rocky peninsula, some 60 feet above Sinclair Bay. Girnigoe Castle was built in the late 15th century, while it is possible to date Sinclair Castle more precisely, in fact to either 1606 or 1607. Remains of both keeps, other ranges of buildings and stretches of curtain walls survive.

The two castles were strongholds of the powerful Sinclair family, earls of Orkney, and later of Caithness, and some research suggests that what appear to be two individual castles were actually always just one fortress.

Visiting in 1760, the Reverend (later Bishop) Richard Pococke described the castles in a letter to his sister. He wrote that "I went to see the castles of Carnigo [sic] and Sinclair, the first situated on a rock over the sea, and separated from the land by a deep fossee, over which there was a draw-bridge... The other is close to it, built for an elder son; in both of them are several apartments, and beyond the first are several little courts on the rocks: Sinclair was built in the time of King Charles the Second, and the King's Arms are on it...This Sinclair was the last of them."

PULTENEY DISTILLERY

Huddart Street, Wick, Caithness KW1 5BA tel. +44 (0)1955 602371 oldpulteney.com

There are three tour options, the pick of which for the more knowledgeable whisky-lover is 'From the Source.'

According to the distillers, "You'll be led by our experienced guide, discovering the journey of our single malt from our water source to your glass. Next, you'll be invited to the whisky tasting room, where you'll explore our core range of single malt whiskies – from our famous 12 Years Old to the deeply warming 18 Years Old – and there's an opportunity to try an exclusive dram selected by the distillery team. Finally, you'll receive a beautiful rocks glass as a gift, so you can enjoy our distinctive single malt at home."

Pulteney is one of those relatively rare Scottish malt distilleries to be situated in the middle of a town, in this case a back street in the Pulteneytown area of Wick. It was established in 1826 by James Henderson, who had previously distilled at Stemster, near Halkirk. After almost a century of operation, Pulteney was acquired by the Dundee blending firm of James Watson & Co Ltd in 1920.

Five years later, Watson's was absorbed into the mighty

▲ *Pulteney distillery.*

Distillers Company Ltd, and in 1930 production ceased at Pulteney, and it remained silent until 1951, when it was in the ownership of lawyer Robert 'Bertie' Cumming. 1955 saw Cumming sell Pulteney on to Canadian drinks giant Hiram Walker and a comprehensive rebuilding programme took place during 1958/59, resulting in the rather 'industrial' external appearance of the distillery today. Allied Breweries Ltd bought Pulteney in 1961, and operated it until what was then Allied Domecq sold the distillery and single malt brand to Inver House Distillers Ltd in 1995.

Two years later a 12-year-old official bottling was released, and that remains the core expression, along with 15, 18 and 25-year-olds, plus the NAS Huddart, with a distinctly smoky profile. A range of vintage bottlings and other limited variants are all available in the distillery shop. The house style is medium-bodied, floral and fruity, with nuts, vanilla and a hint of salt.

'Old Pulteney,' as the popular single malt is known, is produced in a remarkably quirky pair of stills, allied to a pair of cast-iron worm tubs. Both stills boast large 'boil balls,' which encourage reflux, while the dramatically truncated, flat-topped appearance of the wash still is said to have resulted from an incident many years ago when a new still was fabricated for the distillery but turned out to be too tall to fit. The solution was to have a coppersmith remove the top and seal it. There seems to be no proof of this tale, but no alternative explanation for the still's appearance, either, and the roof of the stillhouse has subsequently been raised in height. Well worth a visit just for the stillhouse alone!

The A99 continues from Wick to John O'Groats, where the road west to Thurso and beyond is classified as the A836.

Some eight miles north of Wick, on the shores of Sinclair Bay is the historic fishing village of Keiss, once an important port for vessels in the herring trade. In Frances Groome's Ordnance Gazetteer of Scotland (1882-84) the author notes that Keiss "possesses a boat harbour, with 58 boats and 135 fisher men and boys..." Today, it is still used by inshore fishermen, though the last catch of herring was landed there by local sailors in July 1940.

Near the harbour are the ruins of Keiss Castle, dramatically positioned on the very cliff edge. It was constructed during the late 16th or early 17th century by George Sinclair, the Fifth Earl of Caithness. 'New' Keiss Castle, in private ownership, dates from the second half of the 18th century, but was extensively remodelled in 1860 by David Bryce.

In 2019, Keiss Harbour deputised for Mullaghmore in County Sligo, Ireland, where Lord Mountbatten was murdered by the IRA in August 1979 during filming of an episode of the Netflix royal drama The Crown.

Caithness is home to more brochs per square mile than any other part of Scotland, and their story is told in The Caithness Broch Centre.

THE CAITHNESS BROCH CENTRE

⌂ The Old School House, Auckengill, Caithness KW1 4XP ✆ +44 (0) 1955 631377 ⟨ thebrochproject.co.uk.

Auckengill is located just over three miles north of Keiss, and the centre explores the creation, use and excavation of brochs, essentially drystone towers, with chambers and galleries built into their walls. Brochs were constructed during the last two centuries

BC and the first two centuries AD, and stood up to 50 feet in height.

Close to the Broch Centre is a fine example of the genre, namely Nybster Broch, which comprises a typical stone-built round house and ancillary buildings. It is believed that the site was occupied for more than 1,000 years.

The name John O'Groats (⌀visitjohnogroats.com) immediately conjures up images of charity walks, bike rides and the like, linking this not-quite-northernmost point of Scotland with the southernmost point of Land's End in Cornwall. The distance between the two is 874 miles, and the record for running it is nine days!

John O'Groats takes its name from Jan de Groot, a Dutchman who is believed to have operated a ferry service to Orkney during the late 15th or early 16th centuries. De Groot is said to have charged a groat per trip to ferry passengers to Orkney, hence the name.

With echoes of King Arthur and the Round Table, de Groot built an octagonal house with eight doors and an eight-sided table to avoid arguments over precedence between himself and his seven sons. The site of the house is marked by an earthen mound, close to The Inn at John O'Groats, built in 1875 and featuring an octagonal tower in a nod to the origins of the village.

De Groot is buried in the graveyard at Canisbay Kirk, two miles west of John O'Groats, and the 'John De Groat' stone which formerly marked his grave is now located within the church. Canisbay Kirk is a church with very ancient origins, and the place where the late Queen Mother used to worship while in residence at her nearby home of Castle of Mey (see p.187).

Modern-day John O'Groats may seem slightly underwhelming in terms of architecture and facilities, given the weight of expectation that such an iconic name brings, but the views across the Pentland Firth to Orkney are superb.

One recent addition to the village's attractions is John O'Groats Brewery (⌂The Last House, John O'Groats, Caithness KW1 4YR ✆+44 (0) 7842 401 571 ⌀johnogroatsbrewery.co.uk).

According to the brewery, "Allan, Simon and John have been keen individual home brewers for many years. They started off with kits bought from shops then progressed to all grain brewing using cobbled together ranges of pots and pans in their kitchens and garages.

"The three combined forces with local hotelier Andrew and set up a 4-barrel brewery in the Old Fire Station in John O' Groats in 2015. From there they started producing a range of cask ales, starting by selling bottles locally and then distributing across the north of Scotland. They expanded into the oldest building in John O' Groats, 'The Last House', in 2019, installing a new brewery, bar and visitor centre."

Beers include Golden Groat, Amber Groat, Deep Groat and Swelkie, with Swelkie being named after a local tide that sweeps around the north end of the small island of Stroma.

8 DOORS DISTILLERY

⌂John O'Groats, Caithness KW1 4YR ⌀8doorsdistillery.com

8 Doors is located beside the main car park in John O'Groats, and offers lots to entice the visitor. A range of third-party whiskies bottled for 8 Doors is available, along with the bespoke Seven Sons blended Scotch and Five Ways Liqueur, which combines Scotch whisky, orange, ginger, honey and spice.

These bottlings are available in the visitor centre and shop adjacent to the production area, where stunning views over the Pentland Firth to Orkney encourage visitors to settle down and enjoy a dram or two in the Whisky Lounge, which is open seven days per week for most of the year. Tours of the distillery (Monday to Friday) and tastings are available, while the Whisky Lounge boasts a well-stocked whisky bar, a selection of fine coffees, tray bakes and cocktails, not to mention the chance to sample a Seven Sons whisky coffee.

8 Doors is the work of husband-and-wife Derek and Kerry Campbell, both of whom are local to this part of the county of Caithness, and the quirky name references Jan de Groot's octagonal house.

When it comes to the equipment being used by 8 Doors, a pair of stills was fabricated on Speyside, while the mashing and fermenting kit was sourced from an Edinburgh brewery that was being converted into a garden centre. 8 Doors has opted for lengthy fermentations to create fruitiness, and 'low and slow' distillation. The 1,700 litres' wash still and 1,300 litres' spirit still produce one hogshead-worth per distillation, and because the distillery is right by the sea, the 8 Doors team is expecting a maritime influence from maturation.

The ex-brewery kit came with a mash conversion vessel rather

▲ Casks being laid down at 8 Doors distillery.

than a conventional mash tun, which means it can process grains other than barley. On the long-term 'wish list' is the cultivation of some bere barley [a six-rowed spring barley which dates to the 8th century and is likely to have been introduced by Norse settlers] and have it ground in the local community-owned mill.

8 Doors represents the first licensed whisky-making operation in the John O'Groats area for 180 years, and the 'original' John O'Groats distillery was established in 1826 by George and James Sutherland at Kirkstyle, close to the shore of the Pentland Firth, and near to Canisbay Kirk. It is known that locally-grown bere barley was malted on site. The distillery had a relatively short life, closing in 1838, and today, only a few scattered stones mark the spot where John O'Groats' first whisky was distilled.

A short distance east of John O'Groats via an unclassified road is Duncansby Head, where parking is available adjacent to the lighthouse. There are striking views of Orkney as well as the Caithness coast east and west, but the true delight of a visit

▲ *The stacks at Duncansby Head.*

involves a short walk along the clifftop until the spectacular Thirle Door and Stacks of Duncansby come into view. The Door is actually a large, rocky archway, while the stacks are large, jagged towers of stone, created by centuries of erosion. The rugged coastal landscape teems with birdlife, and provides a peaceful contrast with the bustle of John O'Groats.

Three miles east of John O'Groats by way of the A836 is the Gill's Bay ferry terminal, from where **Pentland Ferries** (✆+44 (0)1955 611 773 ⌖ pentlandferries.co.uk) operates a car and passenger ferry to St Margaret's Hope in South Ronaldsay. The journey takes approximately one hour 15 minutes, courtesy of the MV Alfred or MV Pentalina, and South Ronaldsay is joined to the Orkney mainland by a series of causeways. St Margaret's Hope is located some 15 miles south of the Orkney capital of Kirkwall.

THE CASTLE OF MEY

✉Mey, Thurso KW14 8XH ✆+44 (0) 1847 851473 ✇castleofmey.org.uk.
The castle lies off the A836 west of Gill's Bay, and is best known as being
the Caithness home of the late Queen Mother.

The Castle of Mey was built by George Sinclair, 4th Earl of
Caithness, to a 'z-plan' between 1566 and 1572, and looks out
across the Pentland Firth towards Orkney. The name of the castle
was subsequently changed to Barrogill, and several extensions
were undertaken during the 17th and 18th centuries.

In 1819 the 12th Earl commissioned architect William Burn to
carry out alterations and further extensions in Tudor Gothic style.
The castle passed out of the hands of the Earls of Caithness in
1889, and was acquired by Her Majesty Queen Elizabeth the Queen
Mother in 1952.

The castle was in a poor state of repair at the time, and The
Queen Mother invested in the property and its estate over the
next few years, changing the name back to its original Castle of
Mey. The Queen Mother usually spent three weeks each August
residing at the castle, returning for some 10 days in October. In
1996 The Queen Elizabeth Castle of Mey Trust was established,
and King Charles III is the current president, spending time at the
castle each August, in the manner of his late grandmother.

Visitors may tour the castle itself, and also the landscaped
grounds, including the two-acre Walled Garden, and spend time
at the Animal Centre, located in the East Woods and home to
rare breeds of sheep, poultry, pigs, rabbits, a donkey and even
chipmunks.

The visitor centre contains a shop selling a wide range of gift
items and books, including the Taste of Mey Cookbook, as well as
jam and chutney made from fresh produce grown in the castle
garden, and honey from the castle's beehives. The adjacent
tearoom serves locally-sourced homemade snacks and cakes.

DUNNET BAY DISTILLERY

✉Dunnet Bay Distillers, Dunnet, Caithness KW14 8XD ✆+44 (0) 1847 851
287 ✇dunnetbaydistillers.co.uk

The distillery is a dedicated gin and vodka distillery, set up by
locally-born husband and wife team Martin and Claire Murray in
2014.

The distillery is equipped with two stills, one named Elizabeth

▲ *Dunnet Bay distillery visitor centre*

after the late Queen Mother, who enjoyed her gin with Dubonnet, and the other named Margaret, after Martin Murray's mother.

Dunnet's signature gin is called Rock Rose, and as the Murrays explain, "After fifty-five experiments the final recipe was chosen to give a wee taste of Caithness and the very first batch was distilled on the 17th August 2014."

Visitors are welcome to tour the distillery and its tasting room, with an attractive coastal theme and 'Boat Shed' booths where a tasting of three spirits is accompanied by 'North Coast Stories.' According to the Murrays, "We will provide children with a soft drink and our family activity pack, which guides them through stories associated with the distillery and features our family Miniature Schnauzer dog, Mr Mackintosh, who is the Distillery's Apprentice." A wide range of Dunnet Bay spirits is on sale, including limited edition and seasonal releases.

In 2023, Martin and Claire Murray became involved in the restoration of Castletown Mill where they intend to create a new whisky distillery to be called Stannergill. According to Martin Murray, "The heritage of the building grounds the new Stannergill Whisky in the character of its location. Locals remember working and living in the building and King Charles once said he 'could not bear to see the Castletown Mill become more and more deteriorated.' Exciting times are ahead and I am particularly pleased that we are able to show that historic buildings can be given a new life."

Two miles from the distillery by way of the B855 is Dunnet Head – actually the most northerly point of mainland Britain rather than John O'Groats. This rugged peninsula is home to an RSPB reserve (⌂RSPB Dunnet Head, Dunnet Head Lighthouse, Brough, Thurso KW14 8XS ✆+44 (0) 1463 715000 ⏁rspb.org.uk) where puffins, razorbills, guillemots, fulmars and kittiwakes are common sights by the spectacular sea cliffs.

THE SEADRIFT CENTRE

⌂Dunnet ✆+44 (0) Tel: 01847 821531 ⏁venture-north.co.uk

The centre is situated at the northern end of the two-miles-long beach of Dunnet Bay and its interactive displays and exhibits focus on the wildlife of the area. There is particular emphasis on the seabirds that nest locally, along with absorbing information about the Pentland Firth, the fishing industry, and the whales and dolphins to be found in its waters.

Just over three miles south-west of Dunnet is Castlehill Heritage Centre (⌂Harbour Road, Castletown, Thurso KW14 8TG ✆+44 (0) 1847 821120 ⏁castletownheritage.co.uk). According to Castletown Heritage Society, "It is located within renovated farm buildings immediately adjacent to the cutting yard and quarry of the now defunct flagstone workings. The workings were the first in the country to exploit the commercial possibilities of flagstone and in doing so put Castletown on the global map,"

A Flagstone Heritage Trail brings the local industry to life, and Caithness flagstones can be found all over the world, having been exported from Castletown Harbour as far afield as Australia and South America, while closer to home, The Strand and the concourse of Euston Station in London were paved with Caithness flagstones, such was their reputation for durability.

From Castletown it is just a five miles drive west to re-join the A9 at Thurso.

BIBLIOGRAPHY

Defoe, Daniel, *A Tour Thro' the Whole Island of Great Britain*, 1724-27
Devine, T M, *The Scottish Nation: A Modern History*, Viking, 1999
Goring, Rosemary, *Scotland: The Autobiography: 2,000 Years of Scottish History by Those Who Saw It Happen*, Abrams Press, 2009
Grant, I F, *Highland Folk Ways*, RKP, 1961
Groome, F H, *Ordnance Gazetteer of Scotland*, Thomas C Jack, 1882-4
Gunn, Neil, *Whisky and Scotland*, Faber, 1935
Jackson, Michael (ed. Dominic Roskrow and Gavin D Smith), *The Malt Whisky Companion (8th Edition)*, Dorling Kindersley, 2022
MacLean, Charles, *The Fringe of Gold*, Canongate, 1985
Moffat, Alistair, *The Highland Clans*, Thames & Hudson, 2010
Oliver, Neil, *A History of Scotland*, Weidenfeld & Nicholson, 2009
Pennant, Thomas, *A Tour in Scotland 1769*, Benjamin White, 1776
Pittock, Murray, *Scotland: The Global History: 1603 to the Present*, Yale University Press, 2022
Smith, Gavin D, *An A-Z of Whisky (revised 3rd edition)*, Neil Wilson Publishing, 2009
Smout, T C, *A History of the Scottish People 1560-1830*, Collins, 1969
Taylor, Kenny, *Scotland's Nature & Wildlife*, Lomond Books, 2002
The Statistical Account of Scotland, 1791-99, William Creech
The New Statistical Account of Scotland, 1834-45, Blackwood & Sons

NEWSPAPERS

The Inverness Courier
The John O'Groats Journal
The Orcadian
The Courier
The Press & Journal
The Scotsman
The Stirling Observer

INDEX

8 Doors Distillery 183
A
Abbey Craig 39
Aberfeldy 77
Aberfeldy Distillery 79
Abertarff House 128
Alexander Matheson 146
Alex Fairlie 106
Alistair Stuart MacLean 118
Allanwater Brewhouse 47
Alness 143
Andy Scott 30
Anne, Duchess of
    Hamilton 12
Antoninus Pius 12
Argyll's Lodgings 36
Atholl Country Life Museum
    92
Atholl family 94
Atholl Highlanders 90
Auchterarder 53
Aultlarie Croft 104
Aviemore and Carrbridge
    113
Aviemore Kart Raceway 118
B
Badbea 166
Balameanach 104
Balblair distillery 154
Balhousie Castle 61
Balnagowan Estate 155
Bannockburn Battlefield 32
Battle of Dunkeld 72
Battle of Falkirk 122
Battle of Falkirk Muir 25
Battle of Sheriffmuir 50
Battle of Stirling Bridge 39
Beatrix Potter 70
Beatrix Potter Exhibition
    and Garden 70
Beaufort Castle 141
Beauly and Dingwall 140
Bell's 82
Ben Alder 99
Ben Vrackie 83
Berriedale Braes 167
Birks of Aberfeldy 78
Birnam and Dunkeld 70
Bishop of Caithness, Gilbert
    de Moravia 157
Blackfriars friary 56
Black Isle 139
Black Isle Brewery 142
Black Linn Falls 73
Blackness Castle 14
Black Watch 61
Black Watch Castle &
    Museum 61
Black Watch Memorial 78
Blair Atholl 92

Blair Castle 94
Blair Charitable Trust 94
Blair Drummond 44
Blair Drummond Safari
    Park 43
Blended Malt Scotch Whisky
    152
Blended Scotch Whisky 152
Boat of Garten 116
Bob Dylan 127
Bonar Bridge 155
Bo'ness 12
Bo'ness & Kinneil Railway
    and Museum of Scottish
    Railways 14
Bo'ness Motor Museum 14
Bonnie Prince Charlie 25
Bourbon casks 28
Branklyn Garden 62
Brodie Hepburn Ltd 52
Broomhill 116
Burn Stewart Distillers 46
C
Caddell 45
Cairngorm Brewery 117
Cairngorms National Park
    100
Cairngorm Sports
    Development Fund 115
Caledonian Cana 124
Caledonian Canal 23, 138
Caledonian Railway
    Company 54
Callendar House 24
Callendar Park 24
Camanachd Association 105
Cambuskenneth Abbey 42
Cameron and June McCann
    38
Cameronians 72
Campbell Distilleries 88
Capercaillie 109
Caperdonich stills 28
Carron Company 19
Castle Menzies 78
Castle of Mey 187
Catalina flying boat 144
Charles Edward Stuart 56,
    122
Clan Donnachaidh Centre,
    98
Clan Macpherson Museum
    102
Clann Gunn Heritage Centre
    & Museum 174
Clans & Tartans 130
Colonel Sir David Stirling
    49
Cook & Bernheimer 101
Craigellachie Bridge 21
Cromarty Firth 139, 141
Cù Bòcan 122
Culloden Battlefield 122

D
Dalmore distillery 145
Dalwhinnie Distillery 100
Daniel Defoe 55
Dauphin Francis 18
David Douglas 66
David Douglas Pinetum 66
David M Sutherland 167
David Wilson 60
Deanston Distillery 45
Diageo 101, 139
Distillers Company Ltd 101
Distillers Ltd 52
Donald MacBean 92
Dornoch 155
Dornoch Beach 158
Dornoch Cathedral 156
Dornoch distillery 157
Dornoch Firth bridge 155
Doug Cocker 60
Doune 45
Dounreay 170
Dr Isabel Frances Grant 103
Drumochter Summit 98
Drumossie Moor 122
Duke of Cumberland 36,
    122
Duke of Sutherland 161
Dunbeath 167
Dunbeath Heritage Centre
    168
Dunblane 48
Dunkeld Cathedral 71
Dunkeld House Tree Trail
    73
Dunnet Bay distillery 187
Dunrobin Castle 161
E
Earl of Moray 45
Earls of Mansfield 66
Eden Court 129
Edradour Distillery 88
Elcho Castle 63
Elizabeth Grant of
    Rothiemurchus 113
Ewan 'Cluny' MacPherson
    102
Explorers' Garden 85
F
Fair Maid of Perth 58
Falkirk 19
Falkirk Distillery 27
Falkirk Wheel 29
Fergusson Gallery 59
Forestry Commission 89
Forsyth of Rothes 28
Forth & Clyde and Union
    canals 19
Forth & Clyde Canal 29, 30
Fort William 124
Fotheringhay Castle 18
Francis Groom 166
Frasers of Lovat 128

Fyrish Monument 144
G
Game of Thrones 45
General Wade 99
General Wade's Bridge 78
George Christie 106
George Granville
   Leveson-Gower 161
Georgemas Junction 169
George Stewart 27
Glen Albyn 126
Glenallachie distilleries 52
Glenallachie distillery 52
Gleneagles 54
Glen Mhor 126
Glenmorangie distillery 149
Glenmore Forest Park 115
Glenmore Lodge 113
Glen Ord distillery 139
Golden Eagle 111
Golf 54
Golspie 159
Great Glen 124
Grey Cairns of Camster 175
G.R.O.W 128
H
Harvey's of Edinburgh 107
Helmsdale 164
Highland Clearances 161
Highland Council 103
Highland Folk Museum 103
Highland Games
   Association 135
Highland Wildlife Park 107
Historylinks Museum 156
HM The Queen Elizabeth
   II 29
Holy Rude Church 37
House of Bruar 97
HRH Prince George 165
I
Ian Macleod Distillers 26
Inches 57
Invergordon 143, 144
Invergordon Distillers Ltd
   46
Invergordon Naval Museum
   & Heritage Centre 144
Inver House 155
Inverness 123
Inverness Botanic Gardens
   128
Inverness Castle 125
Inverness Highland Games
   134
Inverness Museum and Art
   Gallery 125
Inverness Victorian Market
   134
Iona 103
Isle of Jura 52
J
Jacobite Cruises 138

Jacobite rising 102
Jacobites 122
James Bond 007 14
James Hamilton, 2nd Lord
   Hamilton 12
James III 42
James Murray, 2nd Duke of
   Atholl 73
James Stuart 56
James V 17
James VI 36
James Watt 13
John and Dorothy Renton
   62
John Balliol 39
John Byset of the Aird 140
John Creed 60
John Dewar & Sons 79, 140
John Duncan Fergusson 59
John Erskine, Earl of Mar 50
John Knox 38, 56
John McCraw 74
John Murray, 4th Duke of
   Atholl 98
Johnnie Walker 139, 163
John Ross 155
Joseph Mitchell 23
J. T. Rochead 41
K
Kaspar Schultz 127
kayak tours 62
Kenny Munro 60
Ken Taylor 127
Kessock Bridge 138, 139
Kildonan Gold Rush 166
King Brude 123
King David 17, 34
King David I 123
King David I of Scotland 42
King Duncan 123
King Edward I 38, 39
King George II 105
King James I 56
King James II 15
King James IV 52
King James V 36
King James VI 18, 55
King Malcom III 147
Kingussie 104
King William I 124
Kinneil House 12
Kirsty and Rami Cohen 93
L
Laidhay Croft Museum 168
Landmark Forest Adventure
   Park, Carrbridge 119
Latheronwheel 168
Leanach Cottage 123
Leighton Library 49
Lieutenant Colonel William
   Cleland 72
Lieutenant General Henry
   Hawley 25

Lighthouse' distillery 154
Linlithgow Distillery 18
Linlithgow Palace 16
Loch Fleet 159
Loch Fleet Nature Reserve
   159
Loch Morlich 115
Loch of the Lowes 75
Loch Rangag 169
Loch Tay 77
Loch Tummel 89
London, Midland & Scottish
   Railway (LMS) 54
Longleat Safari Park 44
Lord Darnley 18
Lovat Frasers 141
LVMH 154
Lybster 174
M
Macbeth 70, 123
Margaret Morris 59
Margaret of Denmark 42
Margaret Urquhart 75
Margaret Wiseman 75
Mark Birkbeck 98
Marquess of Stafford 163
Mary Queen of Scots 15, 16,
   17, 36, 63, 66
Metallica 127
Military roads 21
Millburn 126
Miss Georgina Ballantine 56
Monadhliath Mountains 121
Monty Python and the Holy
   Grail 45
Moulin Brewery 87
Murray Star Maze 66
N
National Trust for Scotland
   28, 72, 73, 92
National Trust for Scotland
   (NTS) 62
National Wallace
   Monument 40
Neil Gunn 168
Neolithic 175
Newtonmore and Kingussie
   102
Niel Gow 74, 94
North Coast 500 138
North Inch 57
North Point Distillery 171
O
Old Town Jail 37
Oliver Cromwell 15, 56,
   124, 149
Oloroso sherry casks 28
Ord of Caithness, Badbea
   and Berriedale 166
Osprey 76, 111
Outlander 15, 45, 141
P
Packhorse bridge 119

Paul Eugene Riley 60
Pernod Ricard 88
Perth 55
Perth Distillery Company 60
Perth Museum & Art Gallery 58
Perth Racecourse 67
Phil Johnson 60
Pitlochry 83
Pitlochry Dam Visitor Centre 84
Pitlochry Festival Theatre 84
Prince Charles Edward Stuart 102
Prohibition 88
Ptarmigan 109
Pulteney distillery 179

Q

Queen Margaret of Scotland 39
Queen's View 89
Queen Victoria 66, 83, 96

R

Red deer 109
Red Grouse 109
Red Squirrel 110
Reindeer 115
Renee MacRae 112
River Beauly 141
River Braan 73
River Carron 24
River Dulnain 119
River Forth 38
River Helmsdale 164
River Ness 124, 127
River Tay 56, 71
River Tilt 93
Robert Burns 78
Robert Graham 56
Robert Stewart of Atholl 56
Robert the Bruce 32, 147
Rosebank Distillery 26
Roseisle 140
Ross & Cromarty 141
Rothiemurchus 113
Rough Castle Experiences 28
Royal Botanic Garden 85
Royal Dornoch Golf Club 158
Royal Zoological Society of Scotland 112
RSGS at the Fair Maid's House 57
Ruthven Barracks 105
Ruthven Castle 63

S

Salmon 84,110
Schiehallion 83
School of Witchcraft & Potions 29
Scone Palace 65
Scotch Whisky 150
Scottish Midland Junction Railway 70
Scottish Railway Preservation Society 14
Scottish Wildlife 108
Scottish Wildlife Trust 76
Scrabster 172
Seadrift Centre 189
Shinty 104
Signatory Vintage Scotch Whisky Co Ltd 88
Simon Fraser 141
Single Grain Scotch Whisky 152
Single Malt Scotch Whisky 152
Sir Andrew de Moray 38
Sir Charles Barry 162
Sir Giles Gilbert Scott 19
Sir Hector Munro 144
Sir Roderick Mackenzie 142
Sir Rowand Anderson 49
Sir Walter Scott 57
Sir William Wallace 39
Site of Special Scientific Interest 75
Skibo Castle 156
Skiing 115
Slochd Summit 120
Speyside Distillery 106
St Blane 48
St Boniface 142
St Columba 71
St Duthac 147
St Duthac's Chapel 147
Stirling 33
Stirling Castle 34
Stirling Gin Distillery 38
Stirling Heads Gallery 36
Stirling Old Bridge 38
St Michael's Church 16
Strathspey Distillery Co Ltd 101
Sunderland flying boat 144

T

Tain and District Museum 147
Teaninich 144
Terroir Distillers 53
The Caithness Broch Centre 181
The Empire 129
The Enchanted Forest 86
The Hermitage 73
The Little Houses 72
The Mound 159
The Northern Meeting 134
The River Tay Public Art Trail 60
The Rolling Stones 127
The Royal Scottish Geographical Society 57
The Snug 117
The Two Battles of Falkirk 24
The Waterlines Heritage Centre 174
The Wolf of Badenoc 71
Thomas Mackenzie 140
Thomas Telford 124, 141, 159
Thompson family 157
Thurso 169
Tim Shutter 60
Tomatin Distillery 121
Tore roundabout 139
Tullibardine Distillery 51
Tummel Bridge 89
Tummel Hydro-Electric Power Scheme 84

U

Uile-bheist distillery 126
Union Canal 30

V

Vikings 164

W

Wade Bridge 22
Wade & Telford 20
Wallacestone Memoria 25
Wasted Degrees Brewing 93
Waterlines Heritage Centre 174
Watermill and Tea Room 93
Wemyss family 64
Westminster Abbey 38
Whaligoe Steps 175
Whyte & Mackay Distillers Ltd 52
Wick 176
Wildcat 110
William Delmé-Evans 52
William Mathieson 149
William McDowel 112
William Wallace 24, 38
Willowgate Activity Centre 62
Wolfburn distillery 170
World Porridge Making Championship 119